Dear Mom & Dad

Thank you for the way you raised me.
You instilled in me a strong work ethic,
a drive to succeed, and an
entrepreneurial mindset.

As a team the two of you created
and implemented a successful business --
something most couples cannot do.

Growing up, watching that experience
was priceless for me. Thank you for
everything you've done for me.

Love,

Jason

Praise for

Heed Your Call

"Using examples from his own journey and those of others, David demonstrates the virtues of embracing *and*—analytics and intuition, empathy and facts, logic and story, art and science— in both your business and personal pursuits . . . The lessons, stories, and ideas that he shares in *Heed Your Call* are meaningful and transcendent . . . something important is happening in this book that will ultimately empower us, individually and collectively, to meet the great challenges that lie ahead."

—Steve Wynne, former CEO, adidas America and
Sport Brands International

"It is not often that someone introduces such a new and fresh currency of inspiration and motivation that creates a road map for anyone to pursue significant change in their personal or business journey. Howitt's book is truly a mashup of today's most contemporary concepts packaged in a unique voice that provokes the idea that expanded consciousness will be the next most important meme."

—Piper Carr, co-founder and chief strategy officer, Citizen, Inc.

"*Heed Your Call* helps us to understand that life is yoga and shows us the yoga of business. In this book, David so eloquently reminds us that we can and must combine love, art, science, and commerce, and that when we do, amazing and meaningful things can and will happen."

—**Tiffany Cruikshank**, international yoga teacher and health & wellness author

"David Howitt believes your life and career should be a spiritual journey, not just a job. His remarkable new book weaves together myth, science, spirit, and business as never before. *Heed Your Call* is gripping, irreverent, and relevant. Read this book. It will change your life."

—**John Kroger,** president, Reed College

"Reading *Heed Your Call*, I realize many of us have been too heedless in our pursuit of success of the American dream. We need to pause and listen, and the first person we should listen to is David Howitt. As we tune in to others like him, we tune in to ourselves and can pursue our dreams more wisely. This is critical reading for entrepreneurs who want to integrate business, purpose, and authenticity for success."

—**John Howard,** founder and CEO, Irving Place Capital

"David Howitt crystallizes the intuitive, demonstrating how tapping into the power within plugs us into the frequency of pure potential and guides us home to ourselves. *Heed Your Call* is an essential toolbox filled with insight, authenticity, truth, and wisdom— a gift toward your personal and professional transformation and to manifesting your true purpose."

—Paulette Cole, CEO, ABC Carpet and Home

"A truly rare and extraordinary book, filled with inspiration and practical wisdom. David Howitt is a gifted business adviser and entrepreneur who fully understands the importance of bringing deep empathy and intuition into our personal and professional lives. This is a must-read book for every person—CEOs, entrepreneurs, MBA students—anyone who wants to enrich their business and personal lives . . . a seamless integration of spirituality, values, and sage advice that will help readers find the perfect balance in work and life. Bring these core principles—this hero's journey— into corporate America and you will make the world a better place to live."

—Mark Robert Waldman, professor, College of Business, Loyola Marymount University, and author of *Words Can Change Your Brain*

"Today's world critically needs the guidance and insight David has laid out in *Heed Your Call* . . . For those who are ready, this book is the formula, encouragement, and incentive needed to empower you to take the next steps on your unique personal journey towards living a fulfilling, inspired, and abundant life. Applying its wisdom could be the difference between monotone versus technicolor existence—the kind of life that can only be realized by living out your truest vision of yourself. David explains how to do it, what you are missing if you don't, and why doing so makes the world a better place.
Be encouraged."

—**Liz Clark**, Patagonia-endorsed professional surfer, captain, writer, spiritual and environmental activist

"Through a poignant interweaving of personal stories, professional anecdotes, and mythological references, David Howitt holds up a megaphone to our inner voice and illuminates why inside of us lies the Holy Grail of happiness. *Heed Your Call* is an honest, nurturing, and inspiring inner travel guide for anyone on the road to discovering their highest purpose."

—**Cali Alpert**, supervising producer, *The Doctor Oz Show*

Heed *Your* Call

INTEGRATING MYTH, SCIENCE, SPIRITUALITY, AND BUSINESS

DAVID M. HOWITT

ATRIA BOOKS
New York London Toronto Sydney New Delhi

BEYOND WORDS
Hillsboro, Oregon

ATRIA BOOKS
A Division of Simon & Schuster, Inc.
1230 Avenue of the Americas
New York, NY 10020

BEYOND WORDS
20827 N.W. Cornell Road, Suite 500
Hillsboro, Oregon 97124-9808
503-531-8700 / 503-531-8773 fax
www.beyondword.com

Project Editor: Henry Covey
Managing editor: Lindsay S. Brown
Editor: Tina Leigh
Copyeditor: Gretchen Stelter
Proofreader: Deborah Jayne
Cover: Devon Smith
Composition: William H. Brunson Typography Services

First Atria Books/Beyond Words hardcover edition February 2014

ATRIA BOOKS and colophon are trademarks of Simon & Schuster, Inc.
Beyond Words Publishing is an imprint of Simon & Schuster, Inc., and the Beyond Words logo is a registered trademark of Beyond Words Publishing, Inc.

For more information about special discounts for bulk purchases, please contact Simon & Schuster Special Sales at 1-866-506-1949 or business@simonandschuster.com.

The Simon & Schuster Speakers Bureau can bring authors to your live event. For more information or to book an event, contact the Simon & Schuster Speakers Bureau at 1-866-248-3049 or visit our website at www.simonspeakers.com.

Manufactured in the United States of America

10 9 8 7 6 5 4 3 2

Library of Congress Control Number: 2013953004

ISBN 978-1-58270-484-5
ISBN 978-1-4767-6714-7 (ebook)

The corporate mission of Beyond Words Publishing, Inc.: *Inspire to Integrity*

To the hero in all of us.
To heeding your call and taking your journey.

I am not what happened to me.
I am what I choose to become.

—C. G. Jung

CONTENTS

CONTENTS

PART III: MASTERY

FOREWORD

"The best way to predict the future is to invent it."

—**Alan Kay**

This book will change your future. In *Heed Your Call*, David Howitt provides us with a road map, one that shows us how to mindfully venture into our future of technology, business, consumerism, and culture. The stories, experiences, and principles collected in these pages not only can, but will, reshape our future.

How do I know all of this? As a technological futurist, my job is to look ten to fifteen years ahead and predict how people will act and interact with technology and interpret the impact these interactions will have on all of humanity. Using a blend of social science, technical research, economics, trend data, global interviews, and even a little science fiction, I envision the futures that we can quite literally go forth and build, modeling the one we will want to live in and contrasting that with the one we will want to avoid. I do this for corporations, governments, militaries, trade organizations, and startup businesses.

This process, called futurecasting, suggests that our future is not a fixed point on the horizon but that it is being built every single day by our actions. These actions are the results of our thoughts. Let me explain why this is.

Right now, we have chips that are fourteen nanometers in size, and as we approach the year 2020, they will be reduced to nearly five nanometers. That is the equivalent in size to twelve atoms placed side by side. In other words . . . it is crazy small.

When intelligence is reduced to such microscopic size, we discover we can turn anything into a computer. We can turn our desks into a computer. We can turn our clothing into a computer. We can even turn our bodies into a computer.

At this atomic level, atoms and molecules are in constant motion and vibration. Their vibrations create energy, and their energy creates things. Our minds are nothing more than a collection of atoms vibrating all the time. Our thoughts originate here, stimulating vibration and ultimately becoming tangible objects and actionable ideas. From this, we can deduce there is no separation between thought and thing. So, being mindful of our thoughts, we can create those things we wish to become the building blocks of our future.

The future is not a result of chaos. It is not accidental. As Alan Kay says, "The best way to predict the future is to invent it." We are the active participants, who through our thoughts, mold and shape it.

Knowing this, we need to ask ourselves: What experiences do we want? What future do we desire? Knowing we are living in a world where we are surrounded by supreme intelligence, both human and technological, what can we best do with these powerful resources?

Einstein once said, "We cannot solve our problems with the same thinking we used when we created them." To build a future of world repair the quest begins within. If we want an existence where the problems of our day begin to fade, we need to mindfully consider why we are doing the work we each do. We must be thoughtful about the relationships we choose to invest in. We need to ask ourselves what we are here to do and how we can best fulfill our life's work. *Heed Your Call* challenges us to commit to inner improvement. It suggests new ways of thinking and encourages us to evaluate the lives we lead today and inspires us to do our part in the collective building of a better tomorrow.

David recognizes on an existential level that we each have a calling; we have gifts to share with the world, and if we do so mindfully, with the highest level of thought and emotion, we can shape a future of an evolved species. We can create a future where our world is repaired, where we operate with compassion, and where what we build and offer in the world serves all of humanity.

In this book, David invites us to embrace and implement eleven principles that have the power to shape the future—tools that we can use to heal the world. They share notable similarities; they are all timeless truths that have been taught to humanity across all cultures and demographics and throughout all time. They have been packaged and delivered via myth, psychology, science, spirituality, religion, and business. David suggests that if we operate with mindfulness, using these tools to guide us, we will begin to operate at a higher level of vibration. As a result, we will raise the bar on tomorrow.

David believes it is our birthright to live happy, enriched, and abundant lives in harmony with one another. We can invent this experience by being mindful and compassionate to others and ourselves and through developing products, services, and technologies in ways that serve our humanity. In doing so, we touch the lives of people everywhere, helping us each fulfill our unique journeys.

The personal tale David shares in *Heed Your Call* is a shockingly honest and heartfelt narrative, not unlike each of our life stories, urging us in our own journeys to be different if we want them to be, to take that moment to choose and change the trajectory we are on and be transformed.

One of the tools he delivers is the power of *and*. He invites us to examine how we can more fully integrate our personal and professional lives, and how we can fuse artistry and logic to evolve products and services that do not succumb to the tyranny of *or*. He believes that when we *include* rather than *exclude*, that is when magic happens. That is when creativity and precision become a winning duality like we've seen in products such as Apple computers and Nike apparel.

Science and technology have progressed to the point where what we build is only limited by the constraints of our imagination. Nothing wonderful was ever built by humans that did not originate from an imaginative thought. In *Heed Your Call*, it is not only conscious companies and entrepreneurs who are highlighted for doing good in the world. David shows us that we all have that ability and that it is time we all engage, that we expand the possibilities of our imagination. As a result, we will not only dream of a radically different future than we have today, we will invent it.

The call to create the world you want to live in is on you. You, with each breath and thought, are building your future self, your future family, your businesses of tomorrow, your community, and ultimately the world. You have this power. And, by the mere fact you are reading this book, there is no doubt you care about your tomorrow. You are invested in the future of our humanity, and you have to make a decision. So, what are you going to do?

There is real power in *Heed Your Call* and a responsibility that comes with reading it. You will know how to transform your business, your community, and your life. You will now know how to invent the future. The only question that remains is, What will you do with that knowledge and that power?

—Brian David Johnson, futurist for Intel

PREFACE

There I was, twenty-two years old, leaving behind my known world. Bags in hand, I stood outside the revolving carousel doors of Chicago's O'Hare airport. Travelers came and went as I stood, frozen in time, contemplating what the hell I was doing. I was leaving. Moving away from my conservative midwestern hometown of Grand Rapids, my fucked up childhood, lifelong friends, and a prestigious internship at a Chicago law firm.

At the time, I wasn't sure what I was leaving it for. All I knew was there was music inside me softly playing, a faint melody percolating, and a voice that was saying, *David, there is more to life than this.* And though the words were not yet resounding—not loud enough for me to know why I was bailing on life as I knew it at least—it was just audible enough to affect me, to urge me to act without much thought.

I am not sure what was calling me to break out of my small-town bubble. Perhaps it was the promise of seeing Heather again, the angel

I had met the previous summer in Colorado (and the woman who would eventually become my wife), or maybe it was the mountains of the West—or maybe it was just the innate need to be disruptive. Whatever it was, something was nudging me to get the hell out of Michigan. I was being pushed in the direction of Portland, Oregon, and my flight into a world unknown to me was leaving in just two hours.

As soon as the flight attendants began to move about the cabin, I ordered a tall Jack and Coke. Never mind how early it was; I needed something to take the edge off. As I imbibed, the liquor poured calm over my emotional cocktail of one part fear, two parts anticipation, and three parts "what the fuck am I doing?" The fellow to my left reading the *Wall Street Journal* was sizing me up, his eyes saying, "Typical college kid, boozing it up in the morning." That was half right—booze, yes; typical college kid, no. I ordered another, and my thoughts began to wander.

David, whether in this life or the next, I will always be with you. These immortal words of my grandmother Lena echoed in my head in my half-awake, half-dream state. As we hummed along at thirty thousand feet, I was transported into a memory from when I was fourteen, when my grandmother and I had stood on the ancient Masada plateau overlooking the Judean Desert. It must have been the blend of whiskey, soda, and uncertainty that conjured up the old memory, but I went with it, letting my thoughts play out some more, walking me back through my upbringing and the only world I had known.

Like a lot of people, my childhood was tumultuous. I grew up in the home of divorced Jewish parents, and being the first-born male, I was forced to grow up quickly. The role I inadvertently stepped into was that of the intuitive, the mediator, the one who always had to make sure everyone else was okay. Much of my energy was spent on concern for the well-being of my brothers and mother. I naturally became the peacemaker, the one who tried to create harmony in the home.

I used a variety of instinctive coping mechanisms to restore calm. One of these I called on whenever my mom was upset and yelling. To calm her down, I would match my breathing to hers. If she was breathing rapidly, I would breathe rapidly and carry on like that for a while. Then, I would deliberately begin to slow each inhale and exhale, and hers would eventually mimic mine. After a while, breathing more calmly, she would lose focus on the source of her frustration, and her anger would cease. Similarly, when I was present during an argument between my parents, I would visualize the room being filled with bright colors. Sometimes it was gold, sometimes blue or green. I would visualize that color pushing out the contention, and the fight would fizzle.

Strapped into seat 7C, I reflected on the memories of my youth. I visualized the same gold light pouring over and silencing my in-flight neighbor, who was now asleep and snoring. It worked.

These intuitive skills were not learned; they were always available to me, even as a young boy. We all have access to them. The gifts of intuition and empathy usually emerge early and reveal to us that we are really more spirit than human. In our known world, which is comprised of the impressions of our parents and our religious, cultural, and academic programming, the skills we intuit show up naturally, prompting us to move forward in our journey. Unfortunately, in our childhood and adolescent years, we are often not attuned to these faint callings. If we are attuned to hearing them, most of us don't understand what they can mean for us. As a result, we get stuck living in the known world, and if we remain stuck, we can't evolve, and as a result, we never fully live.

Whether I was consciously aware of it or not, my spirit refused to remain shackled to the patterning of my youth. It would not let me die old in an expensive tract home purchased with money earned at a stodgy law firm. My seat on United flight 397 to Portland was proof that, by some greater force, I was being thrust into the unknown world that lay in wait. I felt like Dorothy in *The Wizard of Oz*.

Heather's parents picked me up from the Portland airport. Meeting them for the first time, one would have thought I would have delivered a sweaty handshake. Even for me, an event such us this would have traditionally been a source of extreme anxiety. Though she'd be returning to Portland soon, Heather was still in Santa Cruz, where she had been going to school. Our paths had crossed solely because of a mutual desire to attend the Blue Grass Festival in Telluride two summers in a row, and now she wasn't able to be there to greet me with her parents. I typically would have felt a need to impress or put on a show in order to engender love and acceptance. But I didn't need to. Right from the start, we were talking like old friends. There was no reason to explain why I was staying in their home or how Heather and I had connected or the deep soul connection she and I shared. Unconditional love was shining in their eyes and pouring from their hearts. This level of acceptance was new to me, but it felt so comfortable.

In the car leaving PDX, I felt cozy and wrapped in comfort. Fall was approaching, and the entire city was painted in shades of green, yellow, orange, and red. The sky was gray with low, clinging clouds, the kind I would soon grow accustomed to. It was beautiful in its own way and strangely evoked a feeling of home—not the home I had just left behind, but the place my heart wanted to be.

We arrived at their house in the west hills just outside the city. It had started to rain, and I was growing weary. I had been up for hours and the morning booze I had drunk was now giving me a headache. I was invited to make myself at home and was directed to the room where I would be staying. I walked upstairs, changed out of my travel clothes, dove onto the bed, and passed out.

And suddenly, I was back with my grandmother Lena, this time at four years old. She was talking to me in her kitchen, sharing stories about love, compassion, and universal connectedness. It was the first of many times I would hear her use the word *ruach*, which in Hebrew means "breath of God." She was telling me how it was never OK to have hurtful feelings toward another or to make fun of someone different than me. She was telling me the Jews and Palestinians are truly brothers, that despite how most of the world saw it, they were the same. She was explaining to me how, if we stop focusing on our differences and put our attention on *ruach*, we would have more harmony in our lives—and in the world.

Grandma Lena was very wise, and I was especially close to her. She was one of the greatest blessings of my youth. She *got* me when I felt like no one else did. She was an Eastern European Jewish immigrant whose entire being resided in her heart. You could say she was a traditional Jewish grandmother who lived to love. I learned a great deal from her about compassion and being of service, two tools that would forever help on my journey through life. She also taught me about the importance of following my heart and of cultivating the gifts of empathy and intuition I had developed. I am sure it is because of her that I ever attuned my ears to calls from the universe—she was the one who encouraged me to listen.

Like my grandmother, my grandfather was enormously influential. I considered him a hero, a warrior spirit. He didn't try to be like everyone else. He heeded the promptings of his heart and, as a result, lived a full and joyful life.

At seven years old, he arrived on American soil after a chartered boat journey from eastern Russia. He had traveled to the United States with his sister and mother, who were in search of a brighter future. They settled in Brooklyn, and only eight months into their journey, his mother said, "Son, your sister and I are going to Israel. I cannot afford a boat ticket for you but will send for you once I have saved up enough money. In the meantime, I have arranged for your stay at an orphanage." My grandfather, Al Howitt, never spoke to his sister or mother again.

He lived a long and active life, well into his eighties. He never spoke of his mother and the hole in his lineage remained a mystery to us while growing up. After he passed, I took a trip to Israel and through an exhaustive search was able to connect with his sister. She told me a story of how their mother had been raped and ended up bearing a child. That child was my grandfather. After he was born, she tried to love him like her own flesh and blood, but struggled to do so. Raising him was painful because she was constantly reminded of her horrifying past. After years of agony, she felt the only solution was to leave him behind.

Despite being abandoned, my grandfather maintained a heroic attitude all his life, forging on despite the troubles and confusion of the past. Instead of asking the question, *Why is this happening* to *me?* he always asked, *Why is this happening* for *me?* This subtle shift in mindset contributed to his being an excellent father, a success-ful entrepreneur, and an inspiration to his friends and community. Instead of looking for a way out, he looked for strength within and accepted the gifts life offered him.

Though I was 2,281.4 miles from the world I knew so well, I was not alone. The lessons from that familiar place journeyed with me and among them were the principles my grandfather adhered to and Grandma Lena's axioms of oneness and *ruach*. Together we had come to Portland, and they proved to be loyal and comforting companions as I started anew.

Fast-forward eight years later. Ever since first answering the subtle call to leave my known world for the Pacific Northwest, I've expe-rienced the ups and downs of heeding one's call. I've been met with the good and the bad, blessings and blessings in disguise. I've been unemployed, and I've burned the corporate candle at both ends. I've been sick, and I've been well. I've been a starving student, and I've been blessed with abundance. I've experienced joy and suffering, energy and exhaustion. Yet, through it all, I have discovered it is the integra-tion of all emotion, all experience, and all people, places, ideals, and opportunities that makes us so very human, and when we choose to stop and be aware, we experience *ruach*, the breath of God, oxygenating us all. One such opportunity was the sale of Oregon Chai, the company Heather had created and grown from her heart-centered desire to share her chai-drinking experience in the Himalayas with people all over the globe.

When we sold the company, my day-to-day experiences changed significantly as we ventured into yet another unknown world. No longer was I working around the clock, and some financial pressure was relieved. With a bit more time on my hands, life wasn't such a rush, and I became more observant of others and of myself. I was more tuned in to the moment and the desire to know what was to come next. We had two growing children who were well cared for and benefited from the sale by being blessed with the conveniences of life. It was important to me that Heather and I demonstrated balance to them; I wanted to show them how to be in the world and how to authentically give to others, but with each passing day, I was beginning to feel disconnected. Without going to work every day, I was losing my connection with humanity and, as a result, was not a very good example to my kids.

Periodically, I would catch a glimpse of a new business venture on the horizon—a heart-conscious company had started to take shape in my mind. I envisioned it as a business that would support passionate entrepreneurs in their journey, a business to help founders who are creating products, services, and brands that serve the betterment of humanity. I wanted to offer counsel to small business owners. I wanted to support them in effectively bridging the gap between commerce and their heart-centered desires. At the same time, I wanted to share my experience and knowledge about how to build iconic brands that flourish and are recognized for operating in a different way.

Meriwether Group was the company that would evolve from just a spark of an idea—the idea to support founders in fulfilling their journey. In the beginning, I had no clue how the company would be structured, what products or services we would offer, or where the clients would come from. I didn't write a business plan. There was no market strategy to speak of. I didn't have the details figured out, and frankly, I didn't need to. The universe had heard my intentions and was working on crafting the big picture.

As the weeks turned into months, Meriwether began to manifest. I got out of the house and cut back on renovations and long vacations. As I put my attention to this budding company, like-minded principles—such as bankers, lawyers, business partners, and potential clients—started showing up in my professional and personal circles. Together, those who would become my partners and I began to clearly define our mission and structure how our business would operate. We began to put intention around the kinds of clients we wanted to attract. At first, we visualized local brands, those we could build intimate connections with. Later, our client base would span the globe.

It is on those experiences, the lessons learned, the guides and mentors met, and more, that this book is based.

INTRODUCTION

Perhaps you stumbled upon this book because your tactics, mechanisms, and ways of operating in the world are no longer serving you. Maybe you have come to feel, at its most fundamental level, life is meant to be easy, filled with joy, and more fulfilling, yet it is not unfolding as such right now.

You may find yourself saying, "I have a decent job, beautiful children, a nice house, a loving spouse, make good money, and have healthy friendships, yet I feel sad, disconnected, lonely, and tired."

You might find yourself treating discontentment with shopping, eating, binge drinking, or prescription drugs. You may be addicted to social media or television, or you may be having an affair or toiling at a job that is unfulfilling.

Life can be worrisome for many of us. In a world where the national debt has become so large that the debt ceiling is regularly raised, where joblessness affects so many, and where we're some of the most stressed people in the world (in spite of the comforts we enjoy that much of the world does not), many of us are looking for answers. Why are we so stressed and depressed? Why, if we are in possession of creature comforts, education, and support, are we in so many ways struggling?

For many of us—dare I say *most*?—it's a lack of integration. We look at a job market that's sparse, and we say "I have to make money, so I have to settle for whatever comes along." Maybe it's that simple: you feel you can't do something you truly enjoy, let alone love, as well as provide for your family. Then again, maybe you have a job you love, but it still doesn't quite feel like you are executing it in a way that is in line with who you are.

Maybe it's that you feel you can't be a respected executive *and* smoke pot once in a while, that somehow doing so reduces your credibility or puts you in the category of "irresponsible." Maybe you are the scientist who yearns to be a bit of a spiritualist but have been made to believe you can't be both of these things at once. I am here to tell you, *you can*. We are meant to integrate; we are meant to be the artist *and* the scientist, the hippy *and* the executive, the thinker *and* the dreamer—we are meant to live authentic lives, whatever that looks like for each of us.

Whatever the case is and no matter where you are in your journey, you can always break from the confines of your known world and limiting beliefs. To support and help guide you through your journey, this book offers eleven lessons on professional and personal transformation. In the coming pages, you will discover that it is when we accept our unique call and choose to embrace it that a truly fulfilling life is manifested.

Through these eleven lessons, we will be going on a journey—your Hero's Journey. The Hero's Journey is how Joseph Campbell describes the shared experience that is the underpinning for all great stories throughout history, and your story is no different. There are certain stages of the journey that will be familiar but will look different for each and every one of you. In each stage and lesson, you will be learning different principles that will support you on your path and that will bring you to complete your journey in a way that is in alignment with your vision and personality.

By implementing the principles of surrender, trust, manifestation, universal oneness, empowerment, being of service, co-creation, conscious communication, archetypal energies, whole-brain integration, and the power of *and*, you will be able to effectively bridge the gap between where you are now in your life and where you want to be in the future.

We can keep ourselves busy all we want. We can allow ourselves to be distracted and avoid our summons, our dharma, our purpose, but doing so leads to the worst of all possible scenarios—an inauthentic life. But remember, our life is a gift, and I can promise you that when you heed your call and apply these tools, it will be easy, you will see results, and you will have fun along the way. You will feel and *be* connected. You will no longer tolerate living from a place of just coping. You will thrive and transform, and you will be ready for your defining moment.

As you read on, you will be met with a choice, the choice to heed your call or not. If you do, I assure you, you'll be met with the single most liberating and downright life-altering experience you've been confronted with yet—living your life as a modern-day hero. We are all heroes of our own lives. We are all divine and have the capacity to co-create our own destiny, to thrive in a place where we can manifest our dreams.

I tell you this as both the spiritual guy and the executive. I like my green juice in the morning and my tequila at night. I embrace the power of *and* and implement these tools into my journey every single day. As a result, life is easy, fun, rewarding, abundant, and joyful—and yours can be too.

What Makes a Hero

What defines a hero is a curious thing. Many of us grow up thinking that, in order to be great, in order to be considered a hero, we need to become a doctor, a lawyer, a professional athlete, a politician, or some other figure our society considers powerful. The truth is, we can be any of those—or we can be something else. We can be the artist, the musician, the maker of shoes, or the mailman. We can be a web developer, a garbage man, a good parent, or a loving spouse.

My friend Peter is a caretaker of plants. To some, the trimming, watering, and arrangement of plants could seem like a menial task. To Peter, it is his life's work. It is his calling. He is genuinely passionate about their beauty, health, and life-invigorating elements. He pours his heart and soul into selecting just the right plant, its container, placement, and configuration. His eyes sparkle when he works. His voice is rich with excitement when he talks about his passion. Peter is a hero for the service he provides. We all can be heroes—for the service we provide, the way we provide that service, and who we provide it to.

Buddha and Gandhi did not start out as recognized heroes. They were not celebrities or leaders of their community. They were simply men who followed their hearts, became heroes of their lives, and thus became heroes to millions worldwide.

Imagine being born a prince and raised in great luxury. That is exactly how Siddhartha Gautama—better known to many of us as the Buddha—began his life. Shielded from the hardships and suffering of human life, he did not venture outside the palace until he was twenty-nine. Once he saw the living conditions outside the palace walls, he could no longer be content to live the life of a prince, and so he began his journey. The very night he chose to heed his call, he left the palace and his wife and newborn child. He shaved his head, traded his princely clothes for beggar's robes, and adopted a life of austerity. He started looking for answers and so began his quest for enlightenment, which he achieved at the age of thirty-five. He shared his teachings and universal truths with sentient beings for another forty-five years—and ultimately, he still does today.

We see the same with Gandhi, whose life was one of service and ultimate sacrifice. Like Siddhartha, he was born to a family of means. It wasn't until he visited South Africa that he experienced racial discrimination, injustice, humiliation, and disgrace. It was there that he was thrown off a train for refusing to travel in a third-class coach while holding a first-class ticket. The atrocities he witnessed and experienced firsthand encouraged him to fight for peace and equality.

Gandhi spent twenty years in South Africa working to fight discrimination. It was there that he created the concept of *satyagraha*, a nonviolent way of protesting injustice. When later in India, Gandhi's obvious virtue, simplistic lifestyle, and minimal dress endeared him to the people. He spent his remaining years working diligently to both remove British rule from India as well as to better the lives of India's poorest classes. He gave up his comfortable beginnings and committed himself to nonviolently fighting for human rights, ultimately losing his own life at the hands of an assassin.

In all of these stories—my friend Peter and his plants, Gandhi fighting discrimination, Buddha seeking enlightenment, and my inspiration to leave the midwest—there are resounding truths. First, in all cases, we heeded our call. We took a leap of faith to enter the unknown world. Second, we trusted the universe would deliver. And third, we knew no one person's destiny is more important than another's. It is just as important to tend plants as it is to be an activist of nonviolence or a spiritual guru.

The heroic qualities of resilience, the ability to trust in a universal force, and power over tribulation are embedded in our DNA, but they are often undiscovered because of limiting beliefs we develop over time. We are often tainted at a young age by dogma impressed upon us by our parents, teachers, and religious leaders, and their well-intended efforts to protect often cause us to grow into adults riddled with fear and an unhealthy need to control our lives. As a result, we end up barely living; instead, we move through each day chasing money, power, and bigger opportunities or doing all we can to elude harm, pain, and suffering.

Heroes we've read about or seen on the big screen are no different than you and me. They chase power, give way to ego, hide because of shame, and even hold back because of insecurities. Joseph Campbell states that when our lives seem most challenging, that is when we are presented with opportunities to find deeper strength within ourselves. Just like the heroes of the myths we know so well, the challenges we face are the ones we are ready for. "Perhaps," he says, "some of us have to go through dark and devious ways before we can find the river of peace or the high road to the soul's destination."[1] It is through this darkness, through struggle and triumph over tribulation, that we really come to life. It is in that moment that we are most aware of the life we truly want.

How to Read This Book

This book is divided into three parts: Initiation, Your Mentors and Guides, and Mastery. Though the Hero's Journey is cyclical, and often certain stages will overlap or perhaps even come in a slightly different order for you, the book is most clearly understood by reading it straight through. If, within a section, a particular chapter really calls to you, go ahead and honor that call and read that chapter first. Try to at least stay true to the sections, reading the larger parts in chronological order, and if you don't feel a strong pull to do otherwise, reading the chapters themselves in order will be the clearest as well.

As you read, you'll notice the use of *God*, *divinity*, and *the universe*. For our purposes, these terms are interchangeable. I am not talking about a specific god from a specific religion but rather the greater being that you believe in, whether that is a deity, the over-arching organization and power of the universe, or a feeling you get when you think of the source that we all came from. Please insert that concept into your reading whenever you come across one of these words, because this book is about supporting you in *your* journey.

Part I

INITIATION

1

THE ABYSS AND THE ASCENSION

"It is by going down into the abyss that we recover the treasures of life. Where you stumble, there lies your treasure."

—**Joseph Campbell**

The *abyss*. We all know it—that deep, seemingly bottomless chasm of the soul. Many of us have experienced this burden on our spirits at some point in our lives—and for many, those experiences probably took place while at work. I used to be a corporate lawyer, so I know from experience. At the law firm I worked at right out of law school, success amongst partners and associates was solely defined by who could bill the most time. I found myself bogged down in detailed research, writing, and billing time in six-minute increments. I was completely cut off from all human contact, but I thought I was doing what I had to—what was required of me in order to be successful.

Since the eighth grade, every academic and professional pursuit had put me one step closer to becoming an attorney, but when I finally landed the job, only a very small part of me felt I had arrived. As I took a seat at my oversized mahogany desk, only a fraction of me was proud. Amidst the tinge of relief for having arrived was a more pronounced, very real, and truly terrifying sense of dread. There was a black cloud of uncertainty that accompanied me.

While I sat there taking it all in, I thought, *Wait a minute—everything I have pursued for the past twenty years of my life has led to* this? *Is this* really *what I want? Do I* really *want to be dressed in a suit every day, choking on a tie, and numbering my legal pads?* It wasn't until I had exhausted myself for years that I actually stopped to think about whether or not I really wanted to be there. Unfortunately, I very quickly woke to the realization that being an attorney was unequivocally not my calling, that this had all been an act and in no way represented who I truly was. I realized that, up until that point, I had been in service to something that wasn't true for me. I'd been living someone else's idea about what I should be doing—not mine.

On that first day, I was already suffering and went home that night nauseous and thinking, *You're totally fucked, David.* My mind raced with petrifying thoughts: *Everyone in my life thinks this is who I am and that this is what is best for me. In fact, it is what they've all helped me to achieve. My dad paid an exorbitant amount of money for me to attend a prestigious and private law school; teachers pulled strings and wrote glowing recommendations. If I turn my back on this now, I will disappoint everyone.* So I sucked it up, and starting the very next day, I became an actor who, for a year, would play the role of an attorney. I promise you, faking that role is painful. It's tough enough to be a lawyer in a big firm when you legitimately enjoy it, but when you add to that the energy required to "fake it till you make it," it's untenable.

In a law firm, there are partners and associates. Partners are owners of the firm and are the decision makers. They have earned their spot at the top, and once a partner, you become a tenured teacher—or in many cases, a tenured torturer because you have likely spent six, seven, maybe even eight years as an associate earning your rank. Much like being a part of a fraternity, once partner status has been achieved, those who lasted that long are welcome to abuse associates. You might say it's a partner's rite of passage to do so. Granted, the dynamics of firms vary, with some partners being very kind, but generally, they get off on making the lives of associates miserable—it's considered earning one's stripes to get through it.

Unluckily for me, I had to endure some of the "rites of passage" engrained in this particular culture. I won't go into too many details, but an example of a very common law-firm torment occurred at 5 PM on the Friday before Labor Day. All week, I had exhausted my every breath by pulling ten-hour (at the minimum) days. Putting in seventy-hour workweeks is not unusual because you are only as successful as the time you are able to monetize, but in this particular case, I was experiencing an extreme deficit of energy. More than ever, I needed a break. I needed a reprieve from my attorney role. As I was packing up my belongings for the weekend, a senior associate walked into my office and said, "What are you up to this weekend?" Before I could reply, she said, "Actually, don't answer that. *This* is what you are up to," and she threw a huge packet on my desk. It was a brief we needed to respond to ASAP and the research would need to be conducted over the weekend and delivered first thing Tuesday.

I spent the next four days in the office working. At that point in my life, if I had let people see me fail, it would have felt like dying to me. This is not meant to be overly dramatic; failing would have meant my identity and all I knew of myself—all I thought anyone else knew of me—would die, which was not an option for me. So I pressed on, being sure I wasn't "disappointing" anyone.

My emotional suffering was so severe, it was causing my body to breakdown. My stomach was bound in tightly twisted knots, and I was sure my gut lining was plagued with ulcers. After the Labor Day incident, I couldn't take it anymore.

In fact, I was having a nervous breakdown. I was in my very real and terrifying abyss and had to ascend, or I was going to die—not just figuratively but also quite literally if I didn't change the unhealthy trajectory I was on. I was utterly broken and couldn't fake it anymore. I didn't think I could overcome my abyss.

We all use coping mechanisms to overcome our challenges, but we can't and shouldn't overcome our abyss. I realize that sounds crazy, but doing so means we move into survival mode. We use ego-minded techniques, like placating, faking it, and manipulation, in order to get by. These are all strategies we call on to just get through the grind because our ego tells us giving up is not an option. But that is a lie. It is the Protestant work ethic that says life is supposed to be hard and that only those who rise at dawn and put their back into the plow will be seen and recognized. Our culture, society, and government want us to believe this lie because if we do, we create a country where people are too tired to question authority, and when we don't question authority, we can be controlled.

In truth, we do not need to even be in control of our own lives, our own journeys—we need to trust in and relinquish control to the universe. And so we do not need to work and toil and sweat to overcome the abyss. We need to learn to surrender to it. When we surrender, we enter a state of being where we are fully open to possibility, and our guides and mentors can help us ascend. We give up control to universal will, and because of this, we ascend from, rather than conquer, our bottomless chasm. So, finally, eventually, I found myself in a situation where all I could do was capitulate to the divine.

At about 11 PM one night not long after Labor Day, I was still at the office and had to use the restroom. While in the stall, I glanced down and, sitting on top of the toilet paper dispenser, I beheld an industrial-sized tube of Preparation H. It had been squeezed down to the last bit like a roll of toothpaste. Right then and there, I thought, *This is the universe telling me something. It's saying it is time to get the fuck out of here!* During those final weeks leading up to that point, I had become totally disconnected, and every minute at the office felt like an hour. I would stare at the clock and examine how long the day was taking to end. Every morning, I woke filled with dread that I had to do it all over again.

I don't doubt you have experienced exactly what I'm talking about. And to be clear, I am well aware that one person's challenging-in-a-good-way situation is another person's hell, so it's not a judgment on the people who work in those jobs. We're all different, and for me, that night was the turning point that led me out of my abyss. Maybe you've experienced such suffering and have already ascended from your abyss. Maybe you're actually not quite to the bottom yet. Maybe your abyss is the job you're in, the business you started, or the fact that you're currently struggling to find work. Whatever it is, know that it's good that you got there because hitting the seemingly bottom-less pit is the exact thing that needs to happen for you to finally make a change, for you to finally surrender.

For me, when I was in the restroom that night, I knew it was time to leave my situation. My energy shifted. From the depths of doom, despair, and depression, my mind still managed to light up in hope for future possibilities. My breathing changed, and my posture straight-ened. I went home that night and slept like a baby for the first time in nearly a year. It's when you capitulate that you are raw and your spirit is wide open to receive inspiration. As a result, your life can shift in a nanosecond. You can ascend from the abyss instantaneously if that is what the universe wants.

The next morning, I woke with excitement and had a bounce in my step. Even though I still worked at the firm, I knew it was only a short time until I would be moving on. I had told my ego to fuck off and decided that, even if everyone thought I was a loser, I didn't give a shit anymore. I didn't care if my parents were embarrassed about my decision. If leaving the firm meant I would lose all my friends and family, fall off the edge of the earth, and die, then so be it. When I said to the universe, "I'm done. I can't do it anymore. This isn't me. There has to be more than this," the universe heard me loud and clear—and I could have sworn it was relieved I had finally decided to listen to what it had been saying.

That very day, my mentors and guides (which I'll talk more about in part 2) showed up to lead me from my abyss. They began to introduce tools of transformation to guide me through the rest of my journey. Some came in the form of synchronicities, some were ideas, and some were promptings or nudges to do something.

I started talking about my wanting to leave the firm with friends and began putting feelers out for a new job. At that time, jobs were not plentiful in Portland and especially not for someone only a year out of law school with very little other work experience. I put the energy out there anyway. While having lunch with a friend that afternoon, I told him about wanting to change directions, and he told me he knew someone who worked at adidas and that he could pass my info on. I gratefully agreed, hopeful and ready for the universe to help me not just ascend but to flourish now that I was getting out.

When I arrived back at my office, the message light on my phone was flashing. This typically would have filled me with dread because it normally meant a senior partner needed to put me on a research project that would confine me to hours in the law library. But instead, my heart skipped a beat with excitement—it was the CEO of adidas America. I was shocked.

"David, I just got a phone call from a mutual friend and it sounds like we should meet. Call me back and let's setup a time."

I called him immediately, thinking surely it would be a while before we could meet, but much to my surprise, he asked if I could meet with him that afternoon. An hour later, I was on my way to adidas. Our meeting was easy and natural; everything seemed to flow, and I was able to be myself. I was open, honest, and completely relaxed. I left feeling positive. It was an interview unlike any I'd ever had at that point in my life, and I felt like, regardless of its outcome, it was a turning point for me. Things could be easy and happen organically! It was a revelation.

When I arrived back at the office, the light on my phone was flashing. It was the CEO asking me to call him again—and when I did, he offered me a job.

The universe is always working to illuminate our heroic path, and the spark may come at the least expected moment—like the night I stumbled upon the Preparation H. But it is those brief moments in time that invite us to make a choice—the choice to either heed the call or not, to pick up the phone or to ignore it, to surrender to what the universe has planned or to force something that feels unnatural. I've discovered one of the main differences between joyful people and those wrestling with their lives is the joyful bunch not only hear universal calls and impulses, but they also choose to heed them. They even do so regardless of how insignificant the call may seem. Those who wrestle with life and work hard to overcome their challenges are too busy to even notice an impulse or, worse, choose to ignore it when it sounds.

We all too often find excuses that feel like they give us permission to ignore the calls we hear. Obstacles in our way often give us the excuse to throw in the towel; they keep us stuck in our known world, unable to move forward in our journey. Yet, if we succeed in moving past these challenges and accept that they are part of our unique calls, our lives will be much more harmonious and rewarding. We evolve; we expand and are blessed by the universe as we choose to keep moving and growing.

Some of these obstacles will come by way of egocentrism or perhaps pretension, fear, insecurity, fame, or vanity, but no matter what, they are essential to the process; the cycle is not complete without them. These challenges must be surrendered to in order for you to evolve and continue on your path of transformation and reach your defining moment.

DAVID M. HOWITT

The Hero's Journey

The late Joseph Campbell, considered the foremost authority on mythology, found there to be one myth, consistent through all of history, that is central to every religion, spiritual practice, and geographic location. This über myth was first introduced in Campbell's work *The Hero with a Thousand Faces* and is referred to as the Hero's Journey, a term he borrowed from James Joyce's *Finnegan's Wake*. What he tells us is that *mythos* is the collective unconscious reduced to story, and it provides a road map for us to learn and live from. The Hero's Journey is among the most important and powerful of all myths. It is everywhere and central to the most prolific and powerful forces in life. Our journeys, through our lives in general and through our careers specifically, mirror this Hero's Journey. Campbell tells us that the hero's purpose is not as complex as we often try to make it. It is not to save all of humanity, to slay the dragon, to literally save someone's life—at least, it is not *only* these things. It can be as simple as seeking truth, searching for enlightenment (much like you're doing now).

While on the journey, Campbell says the hero will inevitably encounter obstacles. Some of these *are* your abyss, though some may appear as roadblocks on your journey once you are out of your abyss. Once this part of the journey has been completed, the hero can return to his or her community to effectively lead them on *their* journeys. Because of the hero's great actions and wisdom, the tribe as a whole grows stronger and wiser. This is the journey you are now on. As you ascend from your abyss (perhaps even abysses), you will be on the journey to find wisdom and purpose in your work, to realize that you are the hero of your own life.

In a number of popular books and films, such as *The Matrix*, *Star Wars*, and *The Lord of the Rings*, the protagonists go through the very same stages of departure, initiation, and return. In a 1999 interview with Bill Moyers, George Lucas speaks about how the material for

FULFILL
YOUR JOURNEY

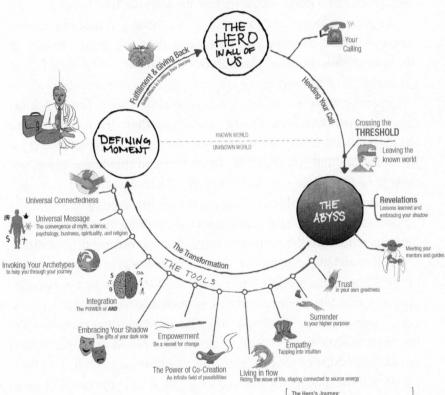

The Hero's Journey:
Joseph Campbell's monomyth, or the hero's journey, is a basic pattern that is found in many narratives from around the world.

Star Wars was inspired by Joseph Campbell's monomyth. During the interview, a number of clips from *Star Wars* are shown that explicitly demonstrate how the film speaks to our individual journeys, and that, if we have a relationship with an energy much greater than us—in the case of *Star Wars*, it is the Force—we can better overcome darkness and move through our transformation.[1] With this in mind, we can see how it is more than mind-blowing visual effects that cause us to become enthralled with these films. It is the relatable stories that connect with us on a deep, soul level that make us diehard fans.

And so we begin our journey, out of the abyss, past our obstacles, and toward becoming a hero—because we all are the heroes of our own stories. Because through the challenges we have all faced, the darkness of hanging on to jobs we hate and relationships that are a drag, these glimpses of hope, of something better, should not be ignored. Most of us have, at one time or another, dragged ourselves through a bad situation, so we can now more fully appreciate the contrast of a rich and fulfilling life. To upshift into that better place, we need to heed the call, step onto the path of our personal journey, and keep trekking, no matter how rugged the terrain becomes.

Remember that, as discussed in the introduction, becoming a hero does not look like any one thing. You do not need to commit yourself to a meditation pillow; you don't need to give up the luxuries of life. There is no need to join a chant circle, believe in a particular god, or move to an ashram. Fulfilling your journey simply requires being open-minded, heeding your call, and integrating these simple universal truths. When you invite them to take hold, you open yourself to the possibility of your life being all you desire.

Now is the time to begin. Heed your call, and set out to fulfill your journey.

2

THE CALL

"The real voyage of discovery consists not in seeking new landscapes but in having new eyes."

—**Marcel Proust**

We've probably all heard someone say they felt they had a calling. Maybe *you* have said you felt you have a calling, but what would you say if I told you we all have calls, and they can happen at many different times about many different things? We all receive calls from the universe, many of them about our work, though some are about our life in general. These faint promptings, these calls that I speak of, are akin to a phone ringing three rooms down. These calls come in an array of forms—a feeling of desperation to leave a shitty job or the suffering caused by a relationship that drains us of our very breath. The call may be a burning desire to take off a corporate hat to replace it with a coach's cap or a dream to leave our small hometown to put down roots in the big city. No matter how grandiose or insignificant they may seem, these calls, these glimpses into our lives that lie in wait, they are real—and they want our attention.

There will be times you may think you hear the ring but aren't entirely sure, and it isn't until you get up and start moving down the hallway that you realize there is, in fact, a call coming through. For some, it will take a lifetime to move toward the source, while others never will. But those of us who swing open the door and answer the call, we are put on our path, unaware of where it will take us but somehow knowing it is where we want to go. When we heed our call, we cross the threshold of our known world and move into the unknown.

The first time I remember receiving a call, I ignored it. I wanted to be an environmental not-for-profit attorney but was told that wouldn't pay the bills. I was programmed to believe work in that field couldn't *really* make an impact. My parents and teachers were always telling me to get good grades, to go to college, and then move on to law school. They told me to become a *real* attorney, one who makes a lot of money. I fell into the trap of believing I needed to keep up with those who defined success as having a prosperous career as a corporate lawyer or doctor. My heart knew that was not what defined success, and neither profession was what I wanted to do, but I chose the path of a corporate lawyer anyway—I refused the call.

I attended Denison University in Ohio and studied all of the courses a law school would want to see in a transcript or that would give me an edge toward becoming a well-paid attorney. While in school, I had a two-year relationship with a young woman. She was an East Coast Catholic girl and fit nicely into my known world, but no matter how right for each other we appeared on the surface, beneath the façade, we lacked soul connection. I deeply wanted to love her, but I couldn't get past the fact that there was a nagging call to break it off—I was subconsciously distancing myself from her.

Our breakup was tumultuous. Everyone thought we were going to marry, including her. No one could understand why I would choose to end a relationship with such a beautiful, intelligent woman, one who I had things in common with and who deeply loved me. Despite the ridicule, the tears, and her broken heart, I listened to my intuition and followed through on my decision.

It was in the spring before graduation, and the universal phone was ringing. This time, I was being called to the West; I thought perhaps to heal from the pain of my breakup. I heard about a bluegrass festival in Telluride, Colorado, that summer, and I knew I had to be there. This time, I heeded the call again, and I enrolled two buddies in the idea of taking a bike trek through the Rocky Mountains.

Our only two commitments were a flight to Denver and an intention to attend the festival. It was antithetical to my nature to go without direction, without a road map or concrete plans. Yet with a bike, a backpack, and very little money in my wallet, I proceeded. Somehow, that summer, I chose to fully heed the call.

We flew into Denver with our bikes disassembled in boxes and hopped a bus. As we made our way through quaint mountain towns, we either slept under the stars or on the floors of the homes of Frisbee throwers we met in parks along the way. In order to get to Telluride, we had to complete one very notable ride over Independence Pass and venture through Aspen. It was an intense climb with multiple switchbacks and an extremely steep incline.

Our arrival into Aspen was shameful. We were covered in dirt and dried sweat but didn't care. All we wanted was food and to appropriately celebrate our victory. I volunteered to buy dinner on my credit card. The smell of rich Italian food and beautiful music lured us to a fancy restaurant. We walked in and were seated immediately. Within seconds of taking our places at the table, our waiter poured us each a tall glass of red wine. Then without ordering a single item, we were brought an incredible spread of food: bread with olive oil and sea salt, salads, antipasto platters, a pasta course, and mains. We were ravenous and enjoying one bottle of wine after another. None of us stopped the celebration to inquire about the endless flow of food that just appeared at our table without us ordering.

We polished off tiramisu, after-dinner drinks, and coffee and then sat back, feeling fat and happy. I was suddenly filled with dread—the feast had to have been brutally expensive. I gulped and asked for the bill. The waiter replied, "Sir, there is no bill. This is our grand opening dinner. You were invited, right?"

I quickly responded, "Yes, of course. I just didn't realize there was no charge." We threw twenty dollars on the table and stumbled out of there laughing. With stars overhead and bellies full of great food and wine, we found a public park to illegally sleep in that night.

When we arrived in Telluride later, the beauty shocked my soul. The majestic San Juan peaks were like nothing I had ever seen, and the smell of mountain air is one I will never forget. We settled into town and ventured into the Fly Me to the Moon Saloon. My buddies and I each grabbed a cold beer and took a seat at a table. I began talking about why I left my college girlfriend and how I couldn't quite put my finger on it, but that I believed there was a woman for me who was going to be everything, the perfect package—beautiful, charming, witty, smart, artistic, and creative. They told me I was nuts, that she doesn't exist, but I was certain she was out there and that I was going to meet her.

We hung out for a while, and then, the most naturally beautiful girl I had ever seen walked up to the bar. She had blond hair down to her butt and a huge smile on her face. Instantly, I felt my heart and soul lighten, as if they were taking off, and I was gasping for breath. I thought, *This is the town. This is the day. And this is the reason for this trip. There she is.* At that point in my life, I wasn't accustomed to that kind of synchronicity. I was not a subscriber to the concept of love at first site or karmic connection, but something in me knew this moment was special, that she was special, that we would be together.

I said to my buddies, "There she is. The girl I was telling you about. That's her. She's glowing. I can see light coming off of her." Mind you, these are words I never used back then, but for some reason, they were just rolling off my tongue. There was no other way to describe her.

One of my buddies replied, "You have to go talk to her. If you really think she's the one, you'll never forgive yourself if you don't at least buy her a beer." It was exactly what I needed to hear.

When I approached, she smiled and introduced herself. Her name was Heather. I felt electricity raise the hair on my arms and every cell in my body knew this was a life-changing encounter. We talked for a while about college, music, and our reasons for being in town. Then, somewhat strangely, I said, "Well, I'm sure I'll see you around the festival." It was odd, but I felt a certainty and calm about seeing her again.

Over the next several days, we continued to bump into each other, but looking back on it now, I shudder to think I left it so open and never made a plan. I had met the girl of my dreams, an angel, and to just say that I'd see her around seems crazy in hindsight—yet instinctively, there was no doubt I would. We ran into each other on hiking trails and amidst crowds of thousands of people. Though I knew I was falling for her, our interactions were entirely platonic. The festival ended, and since this was the pre-cell phone and email era, we vowed to write letters to stay in touch.

I returned home and went straight to work as an intern at a law firm in Chicago to learn the ropes, but from my experience in Colorado, I knew my life would never be the same. What's interesting is that, despite how drawn to Heather I was, I didn't long for her. I felt we were united despite the two thousand miles that separated us. The letters we wrote weren't romantic musings; they were just the stories of our lives. Whenever I would get one from her, pulling the envelope from the mailbox would send the same rush of electricity through me I had experienced the day I met her.

After completing a one-year internship, I planned to attend Lewis and Clark Law School in Oregon. Why the Northwest, where I didn't know a soul? No idea. It's just where I was being led.

Toward the end of the next year, she wrote, asking if I would be in Telluride again that summer. I said yes and that I was sure I'd see her there. Again, very uncharacteristically of me, there was no "I'll meet you there on this day or at this place or at this time," or even just "let's make a plan." I didn't feel the need to say any of that—not in a laid-back, "I don't care" kind of way. I was just sure I would, in fact, see her there.

When I got settled in Colorado, I went for a run on a trail about thirty minutes outside of town. As I was cruising along, I went around a turn, and there was Heather. She had been mountain biking and had gotten a flat tire. I couldn't believe it. She was just as stunned as I was. I hugged her, and in that moment, I knew I was going to be with her for the rest of my life. We walked together, marveling at the universe and catching up while I carried her bike back to town. We spent that night together, and I felt like my life was resting in God's hands. There was never a dialogue about us dating or starting a relationship. It was beyond that. There was no need for words. I told her I had been accepted to law school in Portland, Oregon, and that I would be moving there in the fall. I also shared my apprehension about not knowing anyone in the Northwest and concern for where I was going to live.

I listened in awe as she excitedly told me her parents lived in Portland and she was moving back there from Santa Cruz. The next words out of her mouth were that she would put me in touch with her parents to arrange for me to stay with them until I found a place of my own. This idea seemed ludicrous given that I barely knew her, but intuitively, I knew it was right—that she was right and moving was right. When I returned from Colorado, I booked my flight to Portland. It took me a while, but I was listening to my calls and they were leading me to what would be my home, my wife, and the city where I would finally find my calling.

For those of you who dreamed of being a musician some day but avoided music lessons because you were told you would make little or no money, that was a call you ignored. For those of you who wanted to become a chef rather than a doctor, but enrolled in medical school so your family would be proud, that too was a refusal of your call. If we stop and consider it for a moment, we can all see where we have ignored our various calls.

These yearnings, these calls from the universe, that ring either distantly or crystal clear do so for a reason. They are messages meant to guide us in the direction of our true purpose. Without having this knowledge, it is fair to say we didn't know better—but now we do.

Like you, I've had to endure the shit that we have all, at one time or another, been exposed to. I've had to pay the price of suffering caused by not heeding my call when the phone first started ringing. Part of Campbell's great monomyth, the Hero's Journey, suggests that not heeding our intuitive nudges is a refusal to accept our call, and it causes great suffering. It did for me.

Campbell also says that once we cross over the threshold, it isn't necessarily easy on the other side. As we continue on our journey, it will sometimes be shot in Technicolor and other times it will be shot in black and white. We must all experience dark and confusing times on our journey in order to move toward transformation. And we must travel through the transformation to be led to our defining moment.

During the transformation, we are given tools, and you will find they are instructive and helpful as you fulfill your journey. You may even discover you have received other tools throughout your life, be it the principles of faith, prayer, or others. As we pick up the tools and begin to integrate them into our lives, we may be met with some confusion. We may be forced to examine our behaviors and ways of operating in the world. This self-exploration can cause turmoil and strife, but is never as painful as staying stuck in the known world. As we take our leaps of faith and finally heed our calls, we journey from the known into the unknown.

The Known and Unknown Worlds

Our known worlds are those things that make up our stories. They are our past—and they often define us too much. We tell ourselves that a past event, the way our parents raised us, a state of being was definitive in molding our lives and things simply are that way—we simply are that way. These stories are important to us because they are what we know. This way of being, this type of life, is our known world. Often, our known worlds are familiar to others' known worlds because we find common ground with these stories: We are children of divorced parents. Raised in poverty, raised with money. Grew up in a small town, raised in the city. Dad was a workaholic; dad was a good father. Mom was the breadwinner; mom was the caretaker. Raised by grandparents, raised by one's self. A victim of alcoholism, a child of Christian values. Able to go to college, unable to go to college. These known worlds feel comfortable because we find mutual understanding using them; they feel familiar.

The known world is a perceived safe haven constructed by the influence of our superiors, peers, and a tangled web of limiting beliefs. In the known world, there is comfort in reality that is familiar. Year after year, most of us nestle into this abode, too fearful to ever leave. Within the confines of this familiar place, we limit our potential, which can only be achieved when we surrender to the *unknown* world and set out to live and fulfill our purpose.

But the known—and unknown for that matter—world is not only a very real aspect of our personal lives, it is also just as real in commerce. There are corporations stuck in the known world who refuse to heed their calls. There are those that do heed the call, enter the unknown world, and then get stuck there. Then there are those who start the process of change, who dabble with the transformation, but never reach their defining moment. Then there are companies like Apple.

From an initial spark, from a faint call, it was birthed. Steve Jobs stepped into the unknown world. Board members came along and said he was too young to run it; they pushed Jobs out, and Apple fell into the abyss. Business plummeted and the once genius-led company nearly went bankrupt. It was then that Jobs received another call. He was invited to return to Apple, and he and the brand journeyed through their transformations, applying tools of integration, flow, manifestation, and co-creation. Then, just a few years ago, Apple reached its defining moment. And what's fascinating is, when Apple peaked, Jobs left our planet, as if to say his work here was done.

I too was once in the known world, scared shitless to ever leave. The phone was ringing and I heard the call, but it took years for me to answer and set out to do my life's work, to live my dharma (which is a Sanskrit word defined as "an ideal truth" but also generally means "the teachings that we hold dear"; it is our philosophy). I did not learn from a guru, nor was I a member of any community who subscribed to these beliefs. The themes were always available to me, and I knew it on a cellular level. All of us have access to these truths; we just need to begin to integrate them.

I left my first known world (yes, we go through this more than once, as the process is cyclical) when I journeyed to Colorado that summer and then, eventually, to law school in the Northwest. I left my second known world when I was living in Portland, newly married to Heather. We frequently enjoyed local microbrews, mountain biking, and hikes through the Gorge. I was breathing fresh air and eating incredibly good food. My friendships were genuine, and I rarely missed the midwestern life I had left behind.

Unfortunately, amid my happiness, the law firm was, as previously mentioned, my own personal underworld. Life had become full of stress, long hours, and work that didn't inspire me. I felt that if I didn't leave the firm, I would soon meet the end of my timeline or even worse, see life through, only to be buried alive by depression.

As Portland author Chuck Palahniuk writes in *Fight Club*, "On a long enough timeline, the survival rate for everyone drops to zero," but I didn't want to shorten my timeline.[1] Daily, I'd drag myself into the office, only half-awake because of chronic insomnia. I wasn't any good to Heather as she worked tirelessly to grow Oregon Chai (the business that she had began a few years before). I ate too much, moved too little, and self-medicated with excessive amounts of weed and alcohol. A mix of stress, depression, sleepless nights, and boozing led to a nightly ritual of vomiting. I was "Joe's raging bile duct."[2]

Prior to landing the job, life in Portland had been bliss. I had a beautiful woman by my side, and all was well. I was invincible. That's how the known world can be; sometimes, it's marvelous and full of wonder and excitement. But if we choose to stay there, we don't progress. It becomes a purgatory of sorts, a place where we stop evolving.

Somewhere during those blissful years, ego got the best of me. I started to listen to the known world's cunning and provocative whisperings: "You'll never make money hiking through the Gorge, David. If you're an environmental not-for-profit attorney, you'll be flat broke. You won't be able to buy a house for you and Heather. You won't be able to support her business. How will you ever be able to raise a family? Your friends back in Chicago and Michigan all have homes, David, and wives and families. And here you are, slacking off in the trees and not fucking getting anywhere!"

And I listened to that voice. I allowed myself to believe I didn't have all the tools I needed to thrive as an environmental activist *and* support Heather's vision. I didn't think I could have both. Looking back, I see that wasn't the whole of my life's story anyway. There were more lessons to be learned. But I obeyed my ego. I set my eye on the prizes of money and security and went to work as a corporate attorney.

That is the allure of the known world. When we heed our calls and leap, the known world often beckons us to come back. And perhaps we will be tempted and falter. I took a leap when I got on that plane to Portland, but I faltered when I should have left that job. We can encounter more than one abyss, so it is no surprise that we can hear many calls and have many unknowns that we should jump into. The key is in knowing when we're being held back because of our known world; it is those moments when we are told that we can't have a meaningful job *and* one that makes us happy—even though we can. It is those moments when we hear a voice that says we can't be financially stable *and* inspired—even though that's our destiny.

And now that you have the tools to identify your abyss and obstacles when you encounter them and are ready to hear the calls that are meant for you, it's important to fully understand your own dichotomous nature, so it's clear that we are built to get both what we want and what we need.

3

OUR JANUS NATURE

"We can only learn and advance with contradictions.
The faithful inside should meet the doubtful.
The doubtful should meet the faithful."

—**Shams Tabrizi**

We humans like to think of things in clear-cut categories: black and white, male and female, yin and yang. But we have resistance toward seeing *ourselves* that way. In order to evolve, it is imperative we accept all of our traits—accept that we are good and bad, that we embody both the light and the dark. When we embrace the fact that we possess these opposing traits, we realize we can have those things that seem dichotomous, like inspiration and financial stability, in our lives. This pinnacle moment of acceptance is where we come to next in our journey. Without embracing the dark and the light, we cannot progress.

Meeting Our Shadow

When I first began Meriwether, I hadn't been on the path of company development very long before I felt a strong urge to leave town for several days. I was being energetically nudged into attending a meditation retreat. You would have thought it was the worst time to leave my budding business, but the occasion ended up being right on time, as is always the case when our guides show up to teach us something.

There were fifteen of us sitting in a circle on tufted pillows filled with hulled buckwheat, and the smell of burning incense permeated the room. It was my first time using primordial sound meditation, the method of using a silent mantra to take you into a deepened state of mental calm. Despite gathering with others for family-style dinners and yoga classes, I hadn't spoken to a soul in seventy-two hours. For my meditation retreat, I had selected a weeklong silent retreat at the Chopra Center in San Diego, and that had been a call in itself. It was a process, a series of nudges to explore certain things, both in the world and about myself.

I was happy with my choice to leave behind work and attend this retreat, but there is simply no way I could to have prepared for such an experience, and to this day, I struggle to put into words all that took place. I'll just say the results of my visit ran the gamut from extreme physical discomfort to complete physical bliss. I experienced acute mental clarity, uncontrollable weeping, extreme loneliness, sheer exhaustion, unlimited energy, horrid nightmares, vivid and blissful dreams, and an overwhelming sense of unconditional love. I lived for seven days in a place of complete self-awareness. Words cannot do justice to what such an experience feels like. The whole time I was there, I didn't *do*; I just *was*.

It is curious how, in total silence, the expectations of others fall away. Our expectations of ourselves dissolve as well. I realized how much of our actions and the way we choose to operate in the world stem from a subconscious desire to receive approval from others. During this soul searching, I discovered how frequently we act in order to be validated. But when our ego is no longer being stroked and all we have is our self to be with, validation from others no longer seems important.

My visit to the Chopra Center served as a guide to achieving balance and harmony in my life. The experience of universal expansion took me by the hand, stared me straight in the face, and said, "David, this is the way." During those awakening seven days, I gained tremendous clarity into what the universe wanted for me, how I could best be of service in the world, and how Meriwether would be the ultimate engine to deliver that goodness.

After the weeklong journey, I began to better understand the forces, ideas, laws, and principles that had been applied, knowingly or not, to my life all along. Once these became clear, everything changed. The notion of separateness dissolved, and I could never again return to a place of *other*. I could no longer accept the concept of *or*. Though it took me a long time—about a year—I began to integrate all that I experienced. I learned that when I began to apply these truths, my personal and professional experiences felt more in flow and more harmonious and aligned with greater purpose. The big picture began to look more complete. I was more aware of my actions. Coming nose to nose with my higher self, as well as my shadow, was just the experience I needed. And the universe knew it and had delivered guides in the form of lessons—essential lessons I had to learn before proceeding in my journey with Meriwether.

In Campbell's book *The Hero with a Thousand Faces*, the call to adventure, which I described last chapter as leaving the known world, signifies that destiny has summoned the hero.[1] There has been a transfer of spiritual energy from within the comfort of the hero's known world to an unknown realm that he is destined to travel to. Yet almost always after taking that leap of faith and entering the unknown world, the hero loses his way. The diversions that plague the unknown world can bring great sorrow and suffering, but they also serve to teach important lessons if the hero chooses to see the gifts the lessons bare.

Validating Our Dark Side

Validation of one's shadow is important. When you are alone and on a trip through the mysteries of the universe, this is when your shadow inevitably shows up. It comes barging through the door of your psyche, shouting as loud as a motherfucker in order to get some much-needed attention. In those moments of coming to understand our *True Self* (in universal understanding, this is our soul, our spirit, our highest potential), we are forced to take a hard, honest look at how much of our lives are ruled by our shadow. When we have inner calm and mental clarity, and we have made peace with the dark and nasty parts of ourselves, our shadows, our actions' origins are much more heart centered. They are more authentic. As a result, the outcome of our actions is pure.

While I learned valuable lessons at the Chopra Center, I also evaluated troubling experiences of the past. I became keenly aware that the roadblocks I had endured taught me important lessons. That dreadful year at the law firm, which was nearly unbearable, was just what I needed in order to effectively counsel adidas executives and employees. My experience at the firm was paramount to my future success and to the evolution of those I interacted with.

Just as heroes in stories do, we all stumble. Most of us misinterpret being blessed with challenges as being dealt a bad hand. Our inability to see the bigger picture results from us traveling off our path and getting lost due to unnecessary distractions. These distractions are interests or pursuits that keep us from attuning our ears to the calls of the universe, to seeing the lessons that are right in front of us to be learned. They are the activities and habits we engage in that keep our minds too busy to hear the next right thing to do. Some of these that I struggle with even today are the incessant need to check my iPhone, vapid friendships, and a propensity to overindulge in food. We all have them!

These things in excess do not allow us to tune in to what is best for us; they do not allow us to open up to what good thing is coming next or to have clarity about our lives. Rather, they increase distraction. When we are distracted, we more easily stray from what is best for us—and, ultimately, best for all humanity. However, we must understand that some romping in the forest is part of our journey; it is expected by the universe that we will do so. It is often during these times of diversion that we experience the unraveling of joy by our shadow's cunning. When we lose our way, we are driven right into a head-on collision with our shadow, and that is just what the universe wants. When the self and shadow collide, if we are attuned, that is when we grow. That is when our being truly begins to evolve.

Deep within our psyches lives a draconic collection of traits and behaviors we wish to believe are not a part of us. To most of us, this hidden dragon that is our darker qualities is our greatest foe. By not accepting its existence, it does not disappear. Instead, it breathes fire upon us in order to get our attention. But just like a piano, where the black keys are needed to balance the white, our shadow, the wild assortment of traits and behaviors that are our ego, balances and is balanced by our light within. Without both, we cannot make music. Without accepting the light and dark within us, we fail to be whole and complete.

Many times in life, I have tried in earnest to lock up my ego, to banish my shadow. The more I imprison that part of me, the more it acts out. When we realize that, if we can look at, pinpoint, and label the darkness in others, we are capable of that same darkness as well. By seeing and declaring someone else as being negative (or, on the other side of the coin, as being inspiring), we too have the capacity to be that. One of the greatest lies ever told was that we are not what we see in others.

An acquaintance once said, "I can't stand ignorant people who pretend to know so much." It wasn't long until we were both attending a social event and happened to be in the same circle of conversation. A guest was sharing his thoughts on Mormonism when this acquaintance chimed in, "I think it is a ridiculous Mormon observance to avoid holiday celebrations."

The others in the group politely corrected him by saying that this is an observance of the Jehovah's Witnesses, not the Mormons. Red cheeked and visibly uncomfortable, he tried to save face by saying, "I could have sworn it was the Mormons." This man who had no patience for ignorance had just displayed his ability to be as ignorant as anyone.

We have an amazing ability to deflect our own negative attributes, and we quickly condemn others for the very offenses we commit. So often we are appalled at the inconsideration of a stranger, dishonesty of a friend, or arrogance of a neighbor. We are so quick to expose what we detest in others, yet those very qualities are likely what we hate most about ourselves. The old adage, "When you point one finger, there are three fingers pointing back at you" is so true. Our ego simply cannot bear to admit to being irreverent, rude, or ignorant, and so it projects our perceived ugliness onto someone else.

Most of us have spent years of energy trying to cast away our shadow parts, those behaviors and feelings our ego deems unacceptable. As children, we were taught who we should be in order to deflect pain and be accepted. All opposing characteristics that were not approved of by our leaders were forced into a dark cave within our psyche. This imprisoning of our qualities has done us all a huge injustice. As we force down our perceived negative traits, we unconsciously project them onto others, and it is these others we end up attracting into our lives.

For example, if you were taught lying is bad, you may declare you can't stand liars. Interestingly, you may encounter them at every turn in your personal and professional relationships. All of our lives, our egos have worked tirelessly to save face, to never admit to having unattractive qualities. As a result, our internal realm is disrupted by the perceived negative behaviors of those we interact with—cheating, laziness, bitchiness, or the guy who we think is a total douchebag—easily and consistently disturbing us.

By sending taboo qualities into exile, the subconscious—our reptilian brain, the amygdala—is strengthened. This causes us to operate mindlessly and without control over our actions or feelings toward others. Neuroscientist Joseph LeDoux has focused extensively on the emotion of fear and how our two amygdalae are responsible for actions and reactions that take place as a result of this fear. He suggests, as do many neuroscientists, that the strength of our reptilian brain is often enough to overpower our logical mind. In an illustration, he shares how, if we are at a zoo, peering into the snake den, we know, consciously, the snakes cannot attack us. We are protected either by high walls or inches of bulletproof glass. Yet, if a snake coils and strikes at us, nearly every time, we will leap back in fear.[2] This story illustrates just how powerful our subconscious can be with its shadowiness and irrational fears. If left to their own devices, thoughts and behaviors fashioned from years of programming will override our rational brain. With practice and keen examination of our thoughts, we can avoid functioning from a place where we are trying to avoid scarcity, pain, and suffering, and instead function from a place of mindfulness.

For Carl Jung, the theory of the shadow was his way of conveying the dominant role played by our unconscious. He revealed the problems that can arise if we do not accept the shadow as a necessary part of human consciousness. According to Jung, the shadow includes all the characteristics we are not fully conscious of, every part of our personality that even the ego does not recognize. He says that because our tendency is to reject parts of our personality we dislike, the shadow becomes a dark and negative creature, the monster within. By neglecting these parts, we often sabotage well-intentioned behavior.[3]

Accepting Our Duality

Vedic teachings describe the cycle of birth, life, death, and rebirth caused by karma as *samsara*. So it happens that, when we do not accept the negative parts of us and figure out how to work with them in balance, we relive them out of balance again and again. Sages call this repetition of behavior the *wheel of suffering*. Patanjali, the sage who codified the Yoga Sutras, was a master of consciousness. He recognized that suffering sprouts from the mind and affects our physical, mental, and spiritual well-being. He says that *tapas* is essential to our journey. *Tapas* is defined as "self-discipline" or our "internal fire," and when it burns inside us with intention, it burns away the attachments that are not good for us and sparks the fire of our inner divinity.[4] This means that we can take any situation where something has happened that we are uncomfortable with and find a healthy use for it. For example, we could lose our job but take it as an opportunity to do something new and exciting. Conversely, we could become depressed by feeling rejected and then feel unable to carry on by attaching to it too much. When we become aware and recognize this duality, we are brought to wisdom. We can then consciously destroy ignorance and confusion, and ultimately produce true and lasting happiness.

Bill Clinton is duality incarnate. He is arguably one of the most articulate and talented men to have ever been president, but his behavior, by our societal standards, is quite controversial. Some of us would describe him as being self-serving, crude, and obnoxious, but that is in addition to being charming, gregarious, and full of energy. What we must recognize is these light and dark qualities are closely intertwined. Like within each of us, the seemingly negative cannot exist without the positive and vice versa. Much of the time, the traits that make a person appalling make that very same person appealing.

Clinton's charm and zeal could not exist without his ability to also be self-indulgent and cunning. This is part of what it means to be human. Being in the public eye, his negative traits were in no way shrouded, yet somehow he managed to rise above them. His vulnerabilities are precisely what made him human and relatable. His authentic living and refusal to hide behind his perceived ugly qualities made us connect with him on a deeper level, and as a result, we were more capable of forgiving him.

The late Debbie Ford, a renowned spiritual educator, was best known for her ability to expose the light and dark of our inner realm. She was gifted at taking complex Jungian theories and making these aspects of our human psyche easy to understand. In her books and coursework, she shows how we can release the control of our shadow and be liberated from the hell we bring upon ourselves. By examining and accepting those parts of us we call dark, we bring them to light.

In her book *The Dark Side of the Light Chasers*, Ford shares how our light within is hidden in the shadows of our lifelong narratives. These stories are written by our amassing of childhood programming, beliefs, behaviors, and attitudes. She also shows how our greatest gifts emerge from our shadows; useful wisdom for accepting ourselves and others is woven into our dramatic tales, thus helping us fulfill our journey. In order to make peace with those dark and eerie parts of ourselves, we need to be open to recognizing those traits within. We must learn to embrace all challenges, conflict, and pain. To feel real joy, we must embrace our totality no matter how terrifying it may be. We must begin to accept that what we may have deemed negative can actually serve us well in a time of need. For instance, being assertive, or even (gasp) bitchy, may help to get your kitchen remodeled on time. A touch of self-centeredness could protect you from feelings of resentment. By speaking your truth, no matter how difficult, you are liberated, and your authenticity fosters genuine relationships and greater happiness.

Ford also reinforced the truth that what we rail against only hounds us more. We think if we run from our shadow, we will find peace in our lives, yet the opposite is true. Our repressed shadow chases us. The feelings and thoughts we try hardest to avoid flood our psyches and control our lives. If you are suppressing a lie, arrogance, or selfishness, you will be the first to point fingers at a lying friend, an arrogant neighbor, or a selfish coworker.[5]

When the mind is instructed to repress or repel a trait, it automatically refuses. This is because it can't decipher between *I am* and *I am not* statements. Our minds do not see a difference between *I want* and *I don't want*. Our thoughts only know how to create a vibration. This vibration attracts the content of the subject under attention. If your internal dialogue says, "I don't want my husband to leave me," you will likely attract a spouse who abandons you because the vibration was "leave me." If your thoughts say, "I don't want to be lied to," you may often contend with people who lie to you. Our fears, as irrational as they may seem, vibrate into the collective unconscious. The universe then responds with what we have focused our attention on. It does not hear the words *don't*, *not*, or *no*. It only receives the vibration of the content we have focused on. By sending the universe a vibration of disdain for something, we attract more of it to us because we're stuck on it, constantly thinking about what we don't want. Your life is not happening to you; it is merely responding to your vibration.

Dr. Daniel M. Wegner's Ironic Monitoring Process defines this kind of self-fulfilling prophecy. His process says that when we repress awareness of anything, we invariably hone in on every expression or experience related to that which we repress. He says that when we travel through our journey acting in ways to avoid being criticized, we denounce recognition of our behaviors that should receive criticism. In doing so, we become hyperaware and attracted to anyone who reminds us of those traits we are trying so desperately to deny.[6]

The first step in not trying to avoid these traits, or shadows, is accepting that they are not evil. They are simply misunderstood. In *The Fellowship of the Ring*, Gandalf asks Frodo to carry the ring to Mount Doom. When Frodo asks him why Gandalf can't take it, Gandalf willingly admits that he is weak and has the ability to be corrupted. He is not ashamed of his weakness, but rather recognizes it is simply part of him, and he acknowledges and accepts it.[7]

It is important to understand that without the dark, we can have no light. When we come to understand the dark side and honor its existence, we have the ability to see our path, as it is more clearly illuminated. When Gandalf admitted to being weak and was, therefore, not the right person to take the ring, he was then able to see who should hold the ring and what his own place in that journey was; in the same way, we can see what we should do and what our role is in our own journey when we accept our own darkness.

"Whether you want to believe it or not, you have a dark side," says Deepak Chopra.[8] When you start to ignore it or push it aside, it begins to make decisions for you and strips you of conscious choices. These choices may be as simple as the foods you eat or the words you speak. Chopra warns that our shadow will keep us from being fully, authentically us if we do not embrace it. When we do finally embrace it, we are finally liberated from those behaviors. If we deny ourselves, even just this one side of ourselves, we will soon be overcome by the traits we try so vehemently to deny. Only when we accept all of ourselves can we truly become who we are; "[. . .]the power of wholeness is infinitely greater, and by a miracle of creation it is within your grasp."[9] It is these opposing, and sometimes chaotic, forces that compose the universe and animate our lives. Or as Friedrich Nietzsche put it, "One must still have chaos in oneself to be able to give birth to a dancing star."[10] You must have both black and white keys to make music. You must have light and dark to be genuinely you.

So how do you come to embrace your totality? In my opinion, the best method is through awareness. You must be willing to look within, and own up to the fact that you have the ability to be a liar, rude, or a total shithead. To stop attracting others into your life that hurt you or who have qualities you dislike, avoid focusing your attention on them and their behaviors. Create a vibration for the kind of people you *do* want in your life. Ask to attract those who are respectful, caring, honest, and unconditionally loving. As you do, you will find there will be no room in your life for the others. You just won't see them anymore. If you don't want clients who are perpetually late for meetings, ask the universe for clients who are always on time. If you don't want to have to track down clients to pay their invoices in full, ask for clients who are happy to pay you upfront.

To join hands with and embrace our shadows, Debbie Ford shares a transformative exercise in one of her books. In a state of meditation, she invites us to visualize stepping onto a city bus. As we walk down the center aisle to find a seat, she asks us to take note of the other passengers. Who do you see? Perhaps you notice a disconnected teen, a stodgy lawyer, or a somber elderly man. Maybe you see a meathead or an addict. She suggests that, whomever we see, they are a part of us. She then recommends we give them each a name and, one by one, invite them on a walk. During that walk, we are to ask them what their gift is. We are to ask what it is beneath the perceived ugliness that actually contributes light.[11]

Imagine seeing a passenger who is an artist and is visibly disgusted with the status quo. If you were to invite him on a walk and ask him what gifts he stores beneath his façade of frustration with mediocrity, he might reply, "It has driven me to be industrious. By having disdain for all things average, I have been more creative. I have given myself permission to break the rules." So it is that, when we invite our shadow parts to illuminate the gifts they bear, we can discover, hidden behind banished traits, perks and positive outcomes we have benefitted from because of those shadows. Only once we accept them are we then better able to embrace totality.

As we journey toward acceptance of our duality, the process can be terrifying and painful at times. It can be difficult and uncomfortable to honor all of our ugly and appalling parts. In the process, it's not unusual to go through a bit of an identity crisis. Some of the people we think are our friends may fall away. Destructive yet very enjoyable behaviors and habits we once loved may become increasingly uncomfortable. We may begin to question our own motives. But at the same time, as we continue to call forth the dark and bring it to light, we will be filled with compassion for others—and for ourselves. Over time, people who once annoyed or hurt us will no longer be present in our lives. This is all part of the process of discovering who we are, and I can attest that, when you come through it, you'll discover the temporary discomfort you experienced is nowhere near that of a life lived in darkness.

The Other Side of the Coin

Just as we learn to embrace the shadow, we cannot ignore the light within. The light includes all of our talent, compassion, tenderness, ingenuity, and brilliance. It is all the magical parts of who we are. Too often, we may be so focused on pushing away the dark that we forget to celebrate the light. After a time, we no longer recognize we have these traits. Most of us have a difficult time accepting a compliment. We often allow ourselves to shrink in order to not be recognized. We hoard our gifts and talents for fear of being thought of as a show-off or a know-it-all. The creative, inspirational, delicate, and talented parts of us, when not given a chance to shine, result in insecurity. Not honoring them keeps us from living authentic lives. Just as we see negative traits in others, the greatness, talent, ambition, poise, or beauty we appreciate in another, we also embody. By seeing these positive qualities in another and denouncing their existence in ourselves, we give away our power.

I have always been a people pleaser, the guy who makes sure everyone else is comfortable and having a good time before honoring my needs. I am not alone. You too may be a caretaker, a nurturer, and you may think this is a loving quality. On the one hand, it is, and on the other, it undermines self-love and self-care. By always putting others first, we fail to honor our full potential and our needs. What I came to understand by exploring the teachings of Jung, Ford, Chopra, and others is that people pleasing stems from not feeling cared for. It comes from not feeling good enough. It is the ego whispering, "I don't belong." In order to be seen or to feel like we matter, we bend over backward for others. Doing so further reinforces our feelings of lack because, by constantly doing for others, we deplete all our own energy—and there is nothing left for us.

What we need to do instead is care for ourselves. It is not selfish to take care of ourselves first. If we are not taking care of ourselves, we can't *truly* take care of others, because our aid isn't coming from a place of abundance and acceptance. We have to look inside and embrace both our light and our dark.

We must also learn to identify and call forth the qualities we admire in others. The *I Ching* says, "It is only when we have the courage to face things exactly as they are, without any self-deception or illusion, that a light will develop out of events, by which the path to success may be recognized."[12] Our delusion is what has been holding us back. By believing we do not have the capacity to be selfish (or an asshole) or that we are not beautiful, loved, or brilliant, we cut ourselves off from the ability to reach our defining moment. This is equally as true in our business lives as it is in our personal lives. To become whole and to nurture our authentic selves, we must embrace both our divine and our human qualities. We need to call forward those parts of us we have shunned. There is no human quality we each do not possess. Some may be more pronounced than others, but just because they are not shouting at us, it doesn't mean they are not there.

During my retreat, a mentor at the Chopra Center shared a Cherokee legend concerning the shadow. It is a tale of two wolves as told by a grandfather to his grandson:

"It is as if there are two wolves battling inside each of us. One is good. He is joy, peace, perseverance, love, hope, serenity, humility, kindness, empathy, generosity, truth, and faith. He does no harm. He lives in harmony with all around him and does not take offense when no offense was intended. He will only fight when it is right to do so and in the right way. He saves all his energy for the right fight.

"The other wolf is evil. He is anger, envy, jealousy, sorrow, regret, avarice, arrogance, self-pity, guilt, resentment, inferiority, lies, false pride, and ego. The littlest thing will set him into a fit of temper. He fights everyone, all the time, for no reason. He cannot think because his anger and hate are so great. It is helpless anger, for his anger will change nothing. Sometimes, it is hard to live with these two wolves inside of us, for both will try and dominate our spirit."

The boy looked intently into his grandfather's eyes and asked, "Which wolf wins, Grandfather?"

The grandfather smiled and quietly said, "The one you feed."

4

EMPATHY AND OUR DIVINE NATURE

"The miracle is this: the more we share, the more we have."
—Leonard Nimoy

When I left the known world to journey out West, I had no idea what the future would hold. Though my gut and intuition were telling me my future was there, consciously, I had no idea that I would work nearly a decade as an executive for adidas, that Heather would become my wife, or that she and I would build and sell a successful chai business together. Meriwether was nowhere on the map of my future and neither was meditation or yoga. I couldn't have expected the physical and emotional angst I would endure in my abyss of the law firm or even that I would have worked there at all. I didn't have the foresight to know the identity crisis I would go through after a seven-day silent retreat.

As we reel through our journey, watching the play-by-play of life's experiences, we capture the bigger picture. It is only in hindsight that we see how all the pieces fit together. This can be likened to the weaving of a tapestry. The one who works the loom only sees the side they weave, a gnarled collection of thread. It isn't until their work is complete that they see how those threads create a vivid masterpiece.

The result of heeding your call and entering the unknown world is like that beautiful tapestry. Though you will undoubtedly encounter troubles along the way and fall deep into the abyss, your mentors and guides will lend a hand to help you ascend and return to your path. Once you've found your footing again, you'll travel on, collecting tools for your transformation. As you integrate them into your life, you'll grow, you'll evolve, and one day, you'll bask in your own bliss. For me, the first of the tools I was introduced to was that of our shared divinity, the truth that we are all connected by the cosmos.

Our Shared Divinity

My high school football coach, Coach Barcheski (whom we called Coach Bar), was enormously influential in helping me nurture connectivity with others. He echoed my Grandma Lena's appreciation for oneness. They both shared the belief that all humanity is a single unit, undivided and connected by some greater force. These two prominent people in my life were my greatest teachers. By their examples and beliefs, I came to also believe in oneness, the interconnectivity of us all on a universal level. "There is no *I* in team," Coach Bar would say. And it's true; we are all members of a universal team, here to help each other succeed and live joyful lives. We each bring our unique gifts and contributions to the whole of all beings. We teach, we learn, we give, we receive—or at least, that is the way it is designed to be.

Coach Bar recognized that not only was I a born athlete, but that I also had the instinctive ability to inspire and motivate. He saw in me budding leadership qualities and so invited me to lead our football team. For many, being a leader is synonymous with heavy responsibility. It is a burden. Some even feel being a leader is a bit of an ego fest. For me, neither was the case because I saw everyone—all the players, the coach, the fans, and myself—as parts of the same thing. I was merely a guide to the players, stepping into a leadership role in order to inspire. I simply served as a mirror, reflecting back to them their greatest strengths and weaknesses, to show the team members how to look within themselves for strength and to be the heroes of their own lives. The team responded well to me as their guide. I was the person who could get them fired up. I was able to get them to believe we were badasses and a great team. In the same breath, I could speak about compassion, being of service, remaining humble, and the notion of the humble warrior—being strong and assertive, but not at all costs.

Coach was wise and saw that I also needed guidance on how to better take care of my own emotional and spiritual well-being. He saw that I lived to please others, to make their lives better. He recognized that doing so was admirable but that too much giving and doing for others was leaving my needs unmet. He coached me on how to focus inward and to give to myself with the same level of compassion and love as I gave to others. He assured me that, in doing so, I would be even more effective in my service to others. He was absolutely right. As I cared more for myself, I cared more deeply for the well-being of the team and all people everywhere. And the team felt the appreciation for their various contributions; they felt unconditionally loved, and as a result, their inner peace and happiness rippled out to all the lives they touched.

In our current culture, one of the ways people try to convince themselves they matter, that they exist, is by pointing out how they are different. They think, *If I stand out, if I am different from someone else, then that means I am unique and special. I am alive and real and not alone.* With that thinking, an existential angst gets momentarily quelled. But like Grandma Lena always said, the way to feel connected is not through pointing out the differences but to realize we are all brothers and sisters. We all share the same breath of God, and we all share the same goals.

If you were to travel around the world to watch people pray and worship and then ask them what they are praying for, it would likely be for similar reasons. It would be for the stuff of love, peace, prosperity, and joy. These are the desires of our common divinity.

In order for us to be effective, it is essential we accept the intangible interconnectedness of our human family. Even when we are not able to physically experience this connection, we instinctively know it exists. Each of us has sprung from the same source, crawled from the same primordial soup; we are not all that different. We each have an instinctive drive to see our dreams actualized yet are often met with challenges that cause our behaviors to be incongruent with our goals and passions. When others see and appreciate our true nature and *know* we are part of something bigger and part of a universal connectedness, our path is illuminated, behaviors are realigned, and we are motivated to keep evolving.

Subscribing to this universal truth of our shared collective power is essential to achieving both success and happiness in all areas of life. Having compassion and understanding that we are universally united goes a long way in fostering lasting and impactful relationships. Every human wants to be understood. They want to know someone *gets* them, that they are seen and valued.

When I am tuned in, when my ego is not running the show, this concept of connectedness is integrated into my communications. Our intangible interconnectedness expressed so beautifully by artists has also been supported by discoveries in the world of quantum physics. As reported by Dean Radin in his wonderful book *Entangled Minds*, the appearance of separation is an illusion.[1]

The Science of Our Connectivity

The advancements made in modern physics never cease to fascinate me. Consider energy. It is vibrating all the time, whether we can see it happening or not. These vibrations ripple out to all those around us—and also from city to city, continent to continent, and beyond. These connections and effects of vibration were described by quantum theory and were called "spooky action at a distance" by Albert Einstein, often called the father of quantum theory. Another of the founders of quantum theory, Erwin Schrödinger, dubbed this peculiarity *entanglement*, saying, "I would not call that *one* but rather *the* characteristic trait of quantum mechanics."[2] So "*Quantum entanglement* is a quantum mechanical phenomenon in which the quantum states of two or more objects have to be described with reference to each other, even though the individual objects may be spatially separated." These interactions in the quantum world lead to correlations in the observable world.[3]

So many of us have a hard time grasping the truth and reality of our universal connectivity, and this is certainly for good reason. If we can't see the cosmic entanglement of our energy and vibrations, it is hard to believe it is so. Yet, if we accept it as truth and apply this knowledge to the activities of our daily lives, we become keenly aware of a bigger connection; our day-to-day interactions that once seemed mundane or a struggle will be more powerful, more meaningful, and more effortless.

In an article titled, "Are We Really Made of Stars?" Remy Melina quotes the great scientist Carl Sagan as he explained, we are literally ". . . made of 'star stuff.' . . . We are a way for the universe to know itself. Some part of our being knows this is where we came from. We long to return. And we can, because the cosmos is also within us."[4]

Michael Loewenstein and Amy Fredericks of NASA explain this claim further on NASA's "Ask an Astrophysicist" webpage. When asked about this fascinating subject, they state, "The statement that we are all 'star stuff,' . . . is meant to imply more than that we are made of the same elements that stars are made of. Beyond that, the elements themselves (carbon, nitrogen, oxygen, etc.) were synthesized, cooked up as it were, in the nuclear furnaces that are the deep interior of stars. These elements are then released at the end of a star's lifetime when it explodes, and subsequently incorporated into a new generation of stars—and into the planets that form around the stars and the life-forms that originate on the planets."[5]

So the question about the source of our intuitive wisdom and sense of essential unity is actually based in facts being substantiated by science. We were created with stellar elements, giving us a real connection to each other and the universe at the atomic level. This real connection is not to be ignored, and acceptance and integration of it into your life will have a profound impact on the success and depth of your relationships and business interactions.

My grandfather often said, "Genius is nothing more than knowing what the collective conscious wants before they know they want it." We see this genius occur all the time in entrepreneurship. Take Heather for example. It seemed ridiculous to me, and to many others, that anyone, let alone millions of people worldwide, would be interested in drinking a tea concentrate you could pour from a box. But, by some existential force, she knew they would. Steve Jobs believed, without a doubt and long before people knew it to be true, that the merging of technical functionality with sleek design would take him to the top. Somehow, Jobs knew instinctively that Apple and its integration of beauty and technical brawn would be what hundreds of millions across the globe would crave.

This is the way our collective energy works. The vibrations of our desires, whether conscious or not, are molding the very products and services we have access to today and will enjoy tomorrow. Many, if not most, will call this good luck or timing, but it is more than that. It is our conscious and subconscious thoughts, our energy, and our vibrations that are bringing to the world precisely what we want, when we want it.

The Empathic Field

In science, our energy field, or where we all exist universally, is known as the quantum domain, that level of existence beyond the tangible, beyond matter, an unbroken wholeness in flowing movement. The quantum domain is habitat to all information, energy, intuition, and interconnectedness. It is home not only to that which we cannot see, but also to the more tangible activities of the mind, such as our thoughts, ego, emotions, and some think even memory. Creativity, logic, and resources are also made available through this level of existence. This quantum domain is what we know as the collective consciousness and is sometimes referred to as the *empathic field*. It connects all things. It *is* all things, and there was no beginning to it, and it has no end. You and I are part of this collective and, with this knowledge, have access to pure potential. This collective consciousness is what allows you to tap into the needs of others and provide solutions that you may have not otherwise been able to intuit.

Psychiatrist Roger Walsh, in an article titled "Human Survival," wrote, "The state of the world reflects our state of mind; our collective crises mirror our collective consciousness."[6] We all share existence, and our thoughts and actions—our vibrations—impact all of humanity. You are not isolated and neither am I. When we come to understand our shared purpose and subscribe to the fact that we are all connected, our personal journey and that of all beings everywhere will be profoundly more positive and more life affirming. Alternatively, when we lack self-awareness or a view of the bigger picture, we dull the collective. When we dial up too much of our "left-brain" tendencies and ignore our more empathic and intuitive nature, our relationship with the collective consciousness diminishes. We see examples of this today with corporate corruption, health epidemics, the destruction of financial, civil, and governmental institutions, and the breakdown of communities and families.

An example of collective vibration that can be observed in science occurred in a lab experiment. CIA interrogation specialist Cleve Backster is best known for his theory of primal perception wherein he affirms plants can feel pain and have extrasensory perception (ESP). To take his theory a step further and to help us better connect and resonate with it, Backster began to conduct lab tests using human cells. In one such case, he collected sperm from a donor and placed it in a test tube that was fit with electrodes. The donor was then separated from his sample by a number of rooms. The subject was administered amyl nitrate, a drug that dilates blood vessels in the brain and causes a momentary state of bliss. When he inhaled, the sperm activated wildly; they responded instantly to the donor's euphoric feelings, despite the many walls that separated them.

Backster has conducted similar experiments where he used white blood cells obtained from the mouths of participants. Again, the donors were sent away, in some cases to separate rooms and in other cases miles away. They were fit with cameras and sensory devices to monitor brain activity and then were shown programs that would elicit an emotional response. As he suspected, the human cells in the lab activated during the subjects' emotional surges. The cells would return to a more dormant state when the subjects were no longer confronted with emotionally provoking material.[7]

We are literally masses of energy, and our emotions and thoughts are vibrations. Our very existence commands co-creation and our actualization of greatness in the world. We do this through dharma, our purpose for being, our unique call in life. Living our dharma and walking our path is essential to our happiness and well-being. And since we are universally united, it is also essential to the happiness of those around us. All too often, however, we ignore this calling. We dismiss it as a fleeting thought, despite it being a gut instinct. But our call to do something bigger and better than ourselves is where our true potential lies. The hero always embarks on his journey. He or she always heeds the call, no matter how far off, difficult, or out of character the summons may be. The hero engages and accepts his or her calling with grace and embraces their journey with a sense of purpose and destiny.

In order to have harmony in our personal journey and to experience abundance and happiness in our lives and in our businesses, we need to accept we are more than just flesh. A quote often attributed to French philosopher Pierre Teilhard de Chardin sums it up perfectly: "We are not human beings having a spiritual experience; we are spiritual beings having a human experience."

When you approach your work and relationships with the knowledge that you are part of the collective and that you embody limitless potential, positive change occurs from a place of universal alignment. When you are moving in the right direction, your experiences and interactions are not forced. You will find, the more you subscribe to this way of living, the more your decisions will naturally come from a place of truth and service. They become more meaningful and aligned with your path, as well as becoming more aligned with whom you are engaging. Alternatively, when you do not accept your journey and your calling, you operate from a place of ego. Your ego prefers to be alone and does not play well with others. It isolates itself and prefers separateness, and this fundamentally disrupts our individual and collective awareness.

I always know when I am operating too much in my "left-brain" and relying on ego to drive the day. Since our true nature is pure and united, if we act from a place of ego, we stop evolving, we digress, and we get stuck in a rut—we get stuck in a lone world. Yet when we live in service to our calling, staying rooted in our dharma and seeking universal connection, opportunities flow with ease. We are exposed to those we may never have discovered, a new awareness emerges, and doors open as we heed our call.

In his book *The Spontaneous Fulfillment of Desire*, Deepak Chopra says, "Even when you think you have your life all mapped out, things happen that shape your destiny in ways you might never even have imagined. The coincidences or little miracles that happen every day of your life are hints that the universe has much bigger plans for you than you ever dreamed of for yourself."[8] Time and time again, life has shown me that any intent put toward discovering your calling and of being in flow will open you up to endless possibility. Your life will be shaped and molded by miracles. When you choose to leave the known world to step into your own heroic journey and when you accept there is a bigger consciousness you exist within, your vision will no longer be clouded, and you will more clearly see the path to prosperity. Your relationships and interactions will be more meaningful; you will have a deep desire to be in service to others, and you will manifest projects and opportunities that are enjoyable and fulfilling.

Empathy

Despite how many only see our differences, when we are stripped of our outer trappings—our clothes, the labels we use to describe our skin color or ethnicity, or handy ways to say "you're this, while I'm that"—and shoved into a room together, there is no difference. As we accept this shared divinity, our empathy—another tool of transformation—develops naturally. As we embrace empathy, we are better able to intuit what others are feeling, and we gain cosmic insight into their needs and desires. Doing so helps us to take actionable steps toward supporting them, and as a result, we strengthen our universal team.

Grandma Lena also spoke of an Old Testament Hebrew phrase: *tikkun olam*. This literally translates to "repair the world." Now, most Jews interpret *tikkun olam* to mean philanthropy, which means it suggests that they are responsible for the financial welfare of society. Because of this belief, you often see Jewish children—I know because I was one of them—walking around Sunday school with a collection box. This box is used to collect money for the betterment of the community. What Grandma Lena taught me is that *tikkun olam* is not about philanthropy but about *ruach*—the breath of God. She would say to me, "The way you create *tikkun olam*, David, or the way you heal the world is to return to the *Ruach Elohim*." In other words, when we are in service to others and accept our universal connectivity, it is also when we return to the spirit of God. That is what repairs the world. So life is about service. It is about empathy and knowing we are all one. When we are in service, we see other's gifts and talents. We come to understand other's journeys and that they are heroes of their own lives just as each of us is.

I carried this understanding and practiced these principles throughout all my years in school and still do today. My teachers always said I was a great student but that I would often get bored with academics. Like most kids my age, I wanted to play, to have a good time connecting with others. Our childlike minds get it. We have an inherent need to be out in the world, and as children, we seek every opportunity to connect. As adults, we often hide. We retreat to our desk chairs and the couch in front of the TV. We become intimate with our smartphones and tablets and spend an exorbitant amount of time engaged in activities that steal us away from understanding and being united with others.

Have you ever stood in a public space, such as an airport or mall, and watched the people around you? Try it sometime. For just ten minutes, don't text or update your status on social-networking sites and watch others. I guarantee at least 50 percent of those you see will have their chin glued to their chest and eyes on the digital frame in front of them. This lack of personal connection is dissolving our humanity, and it has to change in order for us to impact our own life and the lives of others in a powerful and positive way.

The urge to make ourselves available to others and to lend a supportive hand is embedded in our DNA. If our relationships continue to devolve, we will fail at honoring our true nature and instincts. The need to be of service, to connect to others, is exactly the reason I felt so compelled, so driven to start my company. I wanted to serve the world by supporting entrepreneurs in their quest.

There have been others in commerce who have shared this same mindset, who have operated with heart and a desire to make other's lives better. Take Steve Jobs for example. He was a brilliant man who operated with heart, and because of this, most people today call him a modern-day hero. His commitment to passion and determination, as well as an intuitive understanding of what consumers want, won him recognition as one of the master innovators of our time, enriching all of our lives. Like Jobs, we all have the capacity for becoming great, for leaving behind our own heroic legacy. It begins with us being heroes of our lives and extending compassion and empathy to all we interact with.

In business, I engage each client as a peer and show I deeply care about his or her dreams and journey. They feel it. They trust me and feel that deep interconnectivity, and they know I have their best interest in mind. They also know that, through my experience and accomplishments in business, they will undoubtedly receive practical and tactile guidance for actualizing their goals and overcoming their challenges.

Susan, an avid yoga practitioner, fell in 2003 when, in a hot yoga class, the towel she was using to absorb her sweat slipped out from under her. The fall resulted in a shoulder injury that took months to heal. As is true with all challenges, there was a silver lining. Through this unpleasant experience, this moment of physical pain, she birthed the brilliant invention of a consumer product that would eventually change the world of yoga forever. This single fall and drive to create a solution led Susan to develop the skidless yoga towel, a mat-sized towel woven from fine microfiber sealed to a layer of small silicone nubs. The patented silicon bottom is what prevents the towel from sliding or slipping on a yoga mat. She branded this towel and founded the company yogitoes in 2004. Within three short years, she and her team built yogitoes into a multimillion-dollar brand and a household name within the yoga community.

When I met Susan in August of 2012, she expressed her desire to sell her company so she could pursue other interests. Throughout that year, I had the pleasure of working with Susan and her team in order to formulate a strategic exit for her that would still support the yogitoes brand. As a result, Susan sold her business quite naturally in a win-win transition to a highly trusted and well-established yoga brand. Throughout our journey together, I immersed myself in her world. I tapped into that universal connectivity to gain understanding of her priorities in life and business, as well as what she hoped to gain through the sale of her company. I listened intently as I worked on constructing solutions. By practicing empathy and universal connectivity, I came to know what the best course of action was, and it flowed with ease.

Ancient sages call this kind of knowledge or clarity *vidya*. It is the knowing beyond what our minds are capable of understanding. In order to make sense of this intangible knowledge, we reference it as intuition or our gut instinct when it is simply pure awareness or pure consciousness. *Jñāna* is the knowledge we attain through learning, from stories, and from the impressions of our parents, teachers, and other influential leaders. Both learned and intuitive knowledge are incredibly valuable when nurturing relationships and constructing solutions for the needs of others—and our own needs as well.

When you can take what you've learned through schooling and from your parents, your therapist, and your religious leaders and weave this knowledge with pure awareness, that is when magic happens. You begin to be able to tap into the desires and needs of loved ones, clients, employees, and colleagues, and instinctively and effortlessly interact with them on a much deeper, more meaningful level. I guarantee, if during your meetings and communications, you engage with a more whole-being approach and remember the truth that we are all one—that we are part of a bigger connection—those you interact with will feel a sense of peace. They will know your vision for them is sound. Often, they will not be able to articulate their comfort, but you will hear it in their voice, see it in their body language, and know by the way they respond to you.

Intuitive Analytics

These mindful and united business interactions have a name in our modern vernacular: *compassionate consumerism*. I often refer to them as *intuitive analytics*, the ability to engage using strategy and logic while weaving in deep empathy and universal connectivity. Utilizing this approach moves us closer to mutually beneficial results.

Put intuitive analytics to the test: In your business interactions, go beyond just hearing what another is saying. Actively *listen* so you can intuitively feel that person's desires, challenges, and dreams. Understand and embrace the notion that comfort during a transition into a new phase of business is more essential than the transition itself. It is not enough to crunch numbers and conduct deep analytical research. Reach deep into the hearts and minds of those you engage with and know what matters to them and their customers. Then, blend heart-centered evaluation with business practicality to make a reasonable action plan for guiding their business and life journey.

Ask your clients thought-provoking and meaningful questions like:

- What is your purpose?
- What drives you?
- What do you feel you are on earth to do?

By asking such questions, you will gain a deeper understanding of the direction their company should go. For example, you may learn that the founder of a gourmet snack company feels her calling in life is to help battered women. By knowing this, you could encourage her to establish a partnership with a local packaging company that enables the snack company founder to package her goods at a reduced cost in order to save money. Then, you could help her set up a system through which the money saved on packaging gets donated as a per-sale percentage to a local women's shelter. Such an arrangement allows the founder to save money on packaging while creating consumer goodwill on behalf of her company. In turn, that feeling of goodwill encourages sales, thus boosting the company's profits, and it all happens while helping the founder fulfill her dream of helping battered women.

Asking these kinds of heart-centered questions helps us be more effective guides and mentors. Doing so also helps us connect, not only with others, but also with ourselves. By checking in, we remain tuned in to the greater purpose of our professional and our personal lives. Do not be afraid to go deep with these questions. The more we are able to enroll ourselves and others in evaluating our intentions and vision, the better off we all will be. When asking these questions of yourself, be still so you can intuit answers about whether or not your pursuits in business—and in your life—are congruent with your heart-centered desires.

Through this process and interaction, by using empathy and having a true desire to know and understand our clients, consumers, and ourselves, we can all be more authentically supported as we fulfill our unique journeys. We can be more mindful about building purposeful businesses that have strong cultures and that can change the way people interact with products and services. We need to remind ourselves, as well as others, of the importance of being fully awake and alive in the world. We need to remember it is essential to our evolution that we move forward in our business dealings in a thoughtful and intentioned way that is in keeping with who we are.

In Someone Else's Shoes

Because we are all made of the same stuff, we each have the ability to seamlessly move into another's breath, into their thinking, and into their emotional state. Doing so is necessary for understanding where they are coming from. It also helps us to not be affected by the behaviors of those around us. It helps us establish and maintain healthy boundaries. I can't tell you how many times I've called on empathy when someone has recklessly passed me on the freeway, hauling ass at ninety miles per hour. In that moment, I could easily think to myself, *What a dick*. But, instead, I use empathy. Doing so allows me to stop thinking about only me. I can instead consider that perhaps the speedy driver has a true emergency and needs to get wherever they are going in a hurry. When I choose to be empathetic, my state of being is not affected, and I do not pass unfair judgment on them.

This tool also serves us well in our business interactions. By stepping into another's shoes, we can tailor our involvement with them while remaining emotionally neutral. We can truly engage with their best interest in mind because we are not operating from a place of *what's in it for me?* Operating from a place of empathy allows us to gracefully accept a client's request to be put on a payment plan when they've never needed to before. Perhaps the reason is some of their hardware went berserk, and they had to shell out ten thousand dollars to fix it, a huge sum of money they weren't expecting to flow out the door that month. Or maybe the client had to dump dozens of pallets worth of boxed chai down the sewer because their co-packer neglected to properly rid the tubes of salsa residue before filling the client's packaging. Empathy allows us to have compassion and patience with a vendor who did not deliver a very important parcel on time. We may never know the delivery guy just lost his wife and had to leave work in the middle of his route, but we can act with empathy instead of jumping to a conclusion that helps no one—such as that he is lazy, doesn't care, thinks his time is more important, etc. How many times have you hoped for a little extra forgiveness for being late or for not executing on a project with precision? Perhaps there have been times when someone looking across the table at you could have made a world of difference in your life and business if they had just been empathetic.

It's by embracing and implementing tools like empathy in our businesses that we have a special opportunity to change the way people interact with each other. Through the distribution of services and products, we have a direct pathway to influencing the world. The intent of business is to create and give value to others, to give people what they deeply desire and what satisfies their needs. Whatever business activities we are engaged in, if we proceed from a place of service and deliver services and products we truly believe in, the impact will be enormous. We can literally heal the world.

Lily, a vibrant twelve-year-old girl, rises early each day. As she enters the kitchen for breakfast, she immediately steps to the sink to scrub her hands. She catches a bit of water in her palms to brush the tops of her feet and behind her neck, a sacred ritual she carries out in the hopes that God will keep her safe and *clean* with her food each day. She does this to be vigilant concerning a very real and severe nut allergy.

At age three, Lily broke out in full-body hives after eating a dinner that included mango salsa. From the reaction, her parents knew it was an allergy and took her to be tested. What they learned is mango and pistachios are in the tree-nut family and Lily had the most severe allergy possible to this group of foods—one so severe, anaphylaxis could threaten her life any time she was exposed.

At eight years old, the life-threatening possibility of her allergy became a terrifying reality. Despite how careful Lily's parents were in selecting the food she ate, she went into anaphylactic shock after eating something mislabeled. She survived, but the experience was so traumatic, her safety became the number one concern of the entire family. No longer would they eat out, all school lunches would be prepared at home, and processed foods were carefully avoided.

Her father, Doug, feeling a deep sense of empathy for Lily's condition, became the point person when it came to mindfulness of her food choices and since her episode, has prepared everything that she eats. When making something new, Doug saves the package label so Lily can read the ingredients and be comforted. Lily loves eggs because they are what she calls an "enclosed food." The shell ensures that the inside has never come in contact with nuts. The same goes for bananas and oranges. The inner fruit is protected by their skin and are her two main snacks. She is on food alert at all times. At school and with friends, she always has her iPhone, knows where the nearest hospital is, and wears a bag with two EpiPens and Benadryl at all times.

Such a challenging existence could have made her bitter and angry. Instead, she is an inspiration. The allergy has helped her become deeply empathetic and compassionate of other children and adults who suffer from sever allergies. In 2010, she and her parents used their challenges as fuel. They set an intention to develop a line of delicious, nut-free snacks, sweets, and chocolate truffles for children like her. Knowing the struggles faced by those with this condition, their mission was to help kids be safe—not just *feel* safe. Don't Go Nuts is the first line of products to launch and is part of multiproduct brand Pinto Barn. From a genuine desire to serve the world, Lily and her parents set this intention and then applied action to bring their products to the market.

The founders of Google also set out with intention. They instinctively knew society needed to have easy access to information. They felt and experienced firsthand the struggles of millions and were called to organize the immense amount of information available on the web, and as we well know, they did just that. One of the founders, Larry Page, states his approach to business focuses not on competition, but rather on transforming products and services that will better ease the pains of the consumer. He believes that you do not achieve outstanding work when you strive to beat another company, but rather when you deliver an experience or product that you authentically feel will make the world a better place.

In an interview with Adam Lashinsky, Page related a story about his grandfather, who was an autoworker. The working environment was so bad that his grandfather would carry a big iron pipe with a hunk of lead on the head to protect himself from the company he worked for. Page remarked, "I think about how far we've come as companies from those days, where workers had to protect themselves from the company. My job as a leader is to make sure everybody in the company has great opportunities, and that they feel they're having a meaningful impact and are contributing to the good of society."[9]

Similarly, when Mark Zuckerberg and his cofounders created Facebook, it was not with the intention to become the world's youngest billionaires. In fact, Facebook was not originally created to be a moneymaking business. It was built to accomplish a social mission: to make the world more open and connected, to unite families, friends, and businesses in a way that reduced undesirable separateness. One of the core beliefs of Facebook is, if people have access to more information and are more connected, value is created in the world.[10]

More small businesses and corporations are catching on to the benefits of bringing their hearts into business. Cascadia Capital is an investment capital group that subscribes to this belief. Unlike most in their industry, they are focused on the transformation that takes place due to an exchange of money, rather than the transaction itself. They have positioned themselves as a peer in the world of finance, rather than an institution. It is nurturing this character and philosophy that has made them successful.

Bryan Jaffe, managing director of Cascadia, said it all comes back to empathy and to really seeing the client and their true nature.

Cascadia is committed to contributing what will ultimately best serve them and their clients. He affirms that, oftentimes, doing what will ensure a win-win situation means giving up a bit of economic gain for the benefits of personal growth and development. He says business owners, no matter what their industry, are more effective when they embrace and practice empathy. It is through this deep connection to each client that trust is established.

Bryan has also said that, all too often, people in finance and investment are too focused on the economics despite a deep nagging letting them know there is more to life than making money. When Bryan shares this message, either verbally or by example, he sees a light turn on in the eyes of the listener. They know it to be true. I once asked Bryan if he thought empathy could be learned. He said he believes empathy is imbedded in our DNA, but we have to learn to manifest it. He is a perfect example of someone who learned to cultivate this important principle. He wasn't always an empathetic businessman. As a matter of fact, he was raised to approach life in a way that mitigated risk.

His grandparents were holocaust survivors, and he learned at a young age to make decisions in order to avoid pain and deflect conflict. This caused him to operate very much from a place of survival and fear. As a result, he ended up functioning as a classic finance undergraduate, working on Wall Street with the mindset to support his experience there. While working the grind, he noticed our financial system creates the vast amount of wealth we see on Wall Street, but it is not achieved by the influence of people. The deals happen regardless of personal touch. This disenchanted him. He wished to operate from a place where an individual's ability to impact the outcome, be it a sale or acquisition, was paramount to the relationship and mutual benefit of all parties. He was tired of seeing personal touch having very little or no impact. This mindset eventually led him to Cascadia, the pioneers of a new paradigm in banking.

To begin to mold and cultivate a more heart-centered approach to your business, Bryan suggests using empathy to walk a mile in the shoes of your client or customer and to do this by really listening to verbal cues and watching for those that are nonverbal. He affirms that, once you see your client's energy shift or a business deal transpire with ease, you know you are on the right path; your empathy is working. He says empathy allows you to look at the individual through a puritan lens versus a capital lens. From there, we are better able to approach situations with a deeper level of authenticity. When we are completely honest on all levels, both with ourselves and the other party, we can more clearly prioritize factors of importance.[11]

Operating from this centered place with empathy and a spirit of service are necessary for tapping into authentic happiness. Our business interactions should be no different. Stop and think for a moment about how you feel when you sell something. It never feels good if you have to force a deal where you know another is going to lose out. If you do, don't you get the sense you are not contributing to the world in a life-affirming way? Consider for a moment what could be possible for you and those around you if you chose to live in your dharma. What would happen if, in your business interactions, you operated with mindfulness and were more focused on the exchange and not the transaction? How much more effective and successful could your life and business be if you stayed true to living in service and to following your journey? I can tell you what will happen—work will be easy, you will have more fun, and you will see positive results.

The most essential principle to embrace in order to be of service and ensure positive outcomes is deep empathy. It happens when, during any interaction, we immerse ourselves in another's life and construct an accurate view of their challenges, desires, and struggles. It happens when we travel through their day and experience their fears and aspirations. It happens when we pause and deeply focus on what it feels like to be them.

Magic happens when we sink into another's life with the intent of having a meaningful conversation about how to create something together that not only gives both parties what they desire, but also creates enough value to upshift all future recipients.

These fundamental truths are so essential to learn and integrate that some business schools are beginning to include the study of mindfulness in their curriculum. They are teaching the importance of being aware of your surroundings, of your impact in the world through life and business, and the inherent benefits of empathy. In some executive education courses, professors offer tools for increasing their focus and guide students through steps to calm their mind. These professors affirm that adopting and implementing these skills is critical for anyone hoping to be successful in an ever-busier environment that is rich with distractions.[12] Mindfulness also plays a significant role in healthy decision making. When your mind is clear and calm, you tend to think through options with deeper care, resulting in more sound decisions. Mindfulness also helps you to listen more intently, which ultimately helps you construct that positive outcome.

Eckhart Tolle, author of *A New Earth* and *The Power of Now* said, "The world can only change from within."[13] Indeed, he is right. This does not only mean from within us individually, but also from within our businesses, our families, and our communities. To be heroes of our own lives and impact change like Buddha and Gandhi, Larry, Peter, and Lily, we must shift our internal framework. We cannot change our personal circumstances, or the world at large, unless we take these universal truths and apply them everywhere, bringing them into all interactions.

Part II

YOUR MENTORS
AND GUIDES

5

THE POWER OF *AND* VERSUS THE TYRANNY OF *OR*:
The Value of Integration

"The intuitive mind is a sacred gift, and the rational mind is
a faithful servant. We have created a society that honors
the servant and has forgotten the gift."

—Albert Einstein

People have said to me, "You know what you are trying to do, David? You are trying to have your cake and eat it too."

And I always say, "You're damn right I am!" I don't know about you, but if I have a cake, I fucking eat it! Having your cake *and* eating it is not wrong. We are meant to do both. At our core, we are creatures of integration, and to bring richness and abundance into our lives, we need to wake up and embrace the power of *and*. We need to have the cake *and* eat it!

Subscription to the cunning and limiting *or* mindset occurs early in our lives. We adopt it through societal pressures and programming from our superiors. We learn to label and define others and ourselves. We believe we can either be in the corporate world *or* attentive, stay-at-home moms, that we can either be a doctor *or* an artist, an attorney *or* a musician, a web programmer *or* a chef. But in truth, we can be all of these, and even all at once if we so choose.

Believing that the scientist is incapable of playing beautiful music or that a heart surgeon can't paint a masterpiece is tyranny, and it limits our potential.

Why is it we define and label each other and ourselves? A great deal of it has to do with the fact that we live in a society that is based on consumer consumption, where people buying things drives capitalism, forming the pillar for our existence. Just as we talked about in chapter 3, we have sharp delineations we use for ourselves, putting ourselves in this category or that one. Hell, we have even labeled ourselves as using one side of our brain more than the other! Though recent science has shown that we always use our entire brain, it can actually be helpful (there we go, showing how much easier we understand labels!) to still think of these qualities as more "left-brain" or "right-brain," as that is where these tasks are typically carried out.

We label "left-brain" thinkers as those who tend to be more business minded. They work in corporate America and are driven by the American dream. As a reward for their hard work, they often consume and collect goods and products such as cars, homes, and toys, where as those with what we may consider to be more "right-brain" characteristics tend to be less concerned with the acquisition of things. They lean toward being more creative types who value culture and art. They tend to spend their leisure time engaged in conversations about how to end world hunger or at the yoga studio or involved in activism. They tend not to consume as much. Those who fulfill "left-brain" roles take on the label of *doer*, *go-getter*, or *corporate worker*. Those who operate with more "right" qualities get thrown into a separate container. They get labeled as *free spirits*, *innovators*, or *creative types*.

Most youth are told that, if they want to succeed, they need to be "left-brain" knowledge workers, they need to be logical and analytical, and they're told that, in adopting these traits, they are more likely to succeed in America. In my son's first-grade class, when the students were asked who in the room would like to be an artist or a musician, more than half of them raised their hands. I bet, if they were asked again in the third, fourth, or fifth grade, there would likely be only a handful of children who would raise their hands. The lop-sided left-brain-qualities-are-more-important dogma is engrained into our psyche at a very young age. It forces us to believe we must choose between being driven and successful or creative and joyful. If you recall, this thinking also contributes to us denying our Janus nature, as we think we are one thing but not the other.

Parents are also responsible for pushing a predefined, "left-brain" mindset as they strive to prepare children to be successful in life. You'll likely agree that if you were to ask most people what their defi-nition of success is, they would say some version of, "Earn a lot of money, have a nice home, get married, raise a family, have enough money to send their children to college with an adequate amount left over for retirement." And we're raised to think this requires what has been traditionally defined as "left-brain" characteristics.

Marpa, an eleventh-century Buddhist master, was also a transla-tor, a farmer, and a skilled businessman. This embodiment of both "right-brain" and "left-brain" characteristics demonstrates he was an integrated man and embraced the power of *and*. He is widely acknowledged to be responsible for having brought the principles of Buddhism to the Tibetan people, and he stood out among other mas-ters because he was both astute and successful in business, yet was a caring father and husband, a teacher to his many disciples, and a spiritual man. He managed to bring together his work and his per-sonal life, melding them into one inspiring life.

As we journey through life and business, the line drawn between being creative and being analytical becomes even more defined. We are brainwashed to believe we must work faster, harder, be more analytical, and have more education than the next guy. We are told to focus on process and systems, detail, logic, results, finance, and numbers. The belief is that, if we do, we will prosper. We will achieve wealth and ascend the ranks. We'll have a bigger title, fancier business cards, a more enticing benefits package, higher compensation, and people will respect us more.

There are many businesspeople and entrepreneurs who have achieved success by balancing these sides of themselves, not only in the way they conduct business, but also in the way they live their lives. Richard Branson happens to be one of these people. In an interview with Gail Lynne Goodwin, Branson stated that it isn't only business that he has been interested in. What he is interested in is "creating things that I can be proud of." He also claims that "being a good entrepreneur isn't really about pounds, shillings, pence, or dollars. They're trying to create a beautiful picture, a vision—something which people love, something which will make a difference in their lives and something they can be proud of. The end result can be that the bills get paid and you build a billion-dollar business. But if you think, 'How am I going to make a billion dollars?' you'll never be successful. Your principal interest has got to be creating something that will really make a difference to people's lives."[1]

What we can glean from Branson's approach to business is that it is not only one of strategy, but it is also an activation of intuition. Branson knows how and when to follow his gut instincts, and when he does, he strikes gold. His uncharacteristic business qualities are what make him one of the most iconic and well-liked billionaires of our day.

The reality is, whether we want to believe it or not, we are each a balance of creative and analytical, artistic and logical, open-minded and more detail-oriented. Each of us is the artist *and* the logical thinker, the hipster *and* the executive, empathic *and* cerebral, brain *and* brawn. The universe, God, the collective unconscious yearns for us to access both sides of ourselves. We bring our best into the world when we simultaneously toggle back and forth between the two. This integration of self is what our businesses need, our relationships need, and what the universe needs.

Howard Schultz is another thought leader and innovator whose business practices are founded on the principles of compassion, value, and service. The book *Onward: How Starbucks Fought for Its Life without Losing Its Soul*, talks about Howard's concern for the well-being of both employees and customers and that this level of care is essential to maintaining the integrity of the Starbuck's brand. Schultz has ensured all employees are offered complete healthcare coverage, as well as stock options and competitive pay. In return, employees deliver a shared reverence for the entire coffee experience to all customers.[2]

Since 1987, when Schultz purchased Starbucks at Pike Place Market in Seattle, the brand and the sacredness of the transition from cup to customer has rivaled its many competitors, and being in service to their employees has earned Starbucks a reputation for being one of the best companies to work for in the world. The way I see it, Schultz recognizes the value of integration. He operates Starbucks from the belief that it pays to not only be focused on profits but on people too. He embodies the "left-brain" quality of wanting to make money *and* the "right-brain" quality of wanting to ensure employees and customers are happy and satisfied.

The Power of Integration

Those who know me know that I'm a successful entrepreneur, that I have money and nice things. They are familiar with the accolades I have received. They also know I am a down-to-earth guy with the seven chakras tattooed on my forearm. They see I have a spiritual practice and meditate and that silent retreats are a part of my life. They also know I am a bit irreverent, that I like green juice in the morning and tequila at night, and that I am not ashamed to admit I really enjoy smoking pot once in a while. They feel comforted by my integrated approach to life and many of them are coming to understand—if I can do it, so can they.

There are those people who will say, "I am more analytical and that is most comfortable for me. I acknowledge my creative side, but I'm not comfortable using it. I may want to practice and learn, but I'm not there yet. In the meantime, I want to surround myself with those who do." I say, good for them! Just acknowledging they have that balance—both light and dark, both creative and analytical—whether they wish to use it all or not, is paramount in achieving happiness. Like their approach to work, I have purposely built the Meriwether team to function in balance. We have those that operate more in the artistic realm and those who are more comfortable in the logical. For any particular discovery meeting, I may decide to engage Julie for her artistry, design, and ethos around brand or Todd, who's highly analytical and a wizard with operations. I am the big-picture visionary, whereas Jake speaks to finance, numbers, and profit. Bringing our skills and strengths together creates balance. This integration of our team is paramount to our success.

Traditionally in business, experts are confined to service silos. This disconnection between consultants can cause founders tremendous suffering that could be avoided with a continuum of services. I'll share a hypothetical story to demonstrate what I mean.

Let me introduce you to Jake Monahan, a landscaper in his early forties who is married to Christy, a stay-at-home mom. They have two boys, ages eleven and thirteen, and they all experience daily turmoil over the loss of Angela, the eldest child who was the victim of a fatal, texting-induced crash last year. This family struggles to extend forgiveness, rather than rage, toward the twenty-seven-year-old man who veered into head-on traffic, taking Angela's life yet miraculously walking away from the tragedy with only a few broken bones.

This instantaneous and tragic turn of events changed the Monahans' lives forever. In order to somehow make a wrong right, Jake and

Christy vowed to pour all of their energy and life savings into manufacturing a device that would automatically deactivate cell phones in every manufactured vehicle. I can relate; if I had lost one of my children due to a crash caused by texting, I would have probably pursued the same mission.

To raise money, Jake and Christy decide to request donations from friends, family, and supporters in their community. They hold fund-raising events at local schools and churches every weekend for months, but after exhausting all their resources, the sum raised is thirty-seven thousand dollars, barely enough to pay them for their time to conduct research and development. They know they need significantly more capital, so they scrape by on the little they have to build an investment brief to present to a private equity group.

Upon arrival at the VC firm, they shake hands with Steve, an angel investor whose net worth exceeds seventy million dollars. He's been investing and reaping the benefits of others success for over thirty years. Steve is divorced and doesn't have children. He will never know the pain the Monahans have suffered, yet he manages to comfort them with expertise and agrees to invest. Steve can see how this product could potentially make him a ton of money if it were brought to market through auto manufacturers. To him, it's about profits. This is the first day in the Monahans' journey of launching a start-up where Angela will begin to fade into the background.

Steve refers the vulnerable couple to a colleague's law firm. They receive guidance in setting up their new business entity and reluctantly listen to an exhaustive list of possible liability scenarios. The attorney shares these potential atrocities so the naïve couple will know how to protect themselves in a legal bind. The attorney is like most—persuasive—and he fills the Monahans with fear. They become terrified by the possibility of losing everything in an effort to protect others on the road, but now see that could be a reality if the product they produce is faulty and results in another fatal crash.

They hire the legal advisory team who also persuades the couple into having them and the angel investor function as the Monahans' board of advisors. Due to the combined sizable investment of the counsel team and Steve, the board becomes the majority equity partners. Angela has become lost in the dealings, and now Jake and Christy begin to fade as well.

With significant funding available, the board hires a powerful advertising and PR firm, who also happen to represent two automakers. On the surface, this seems to be beneficial, but what Jake and Christy don't realize is the staff of this agency is not concerned with the Monahans' loss, and since the board of advisors has hired a resource to be a liaison between them and the firm, the weakening couple never even meet those driving PR. What's ironic is everyone, except Jake and Christy, are frequently texting each other on their drives home from the office.

As the Monahans' company grows, much without their involvement, it is eventually positioned to sell, and the buyer happens to be one of the largest auto manufacturers in America. The selling price? One hundred and thirty million dollars. When it comes time to talk about where Jake and Christy would like dividends to be allocated, having never lost sight of their reason for starting this business, they say they want a significant portion to be used for a nonprofit. Their mission is to have the organization fund medical treatment for children who are surviving victims of car crashes. Their desire is dismissed and their hearts are broken. What began as a soulful desire to make driving safer and a mission to somehow undo the wrong done to their family, became a heartless and profit-driven venture.

Unfortunately, many in commerce operate with their eyes on this type of prize. They do not bring their hearts to the boardroom or practice empathy when they first struggle to find common ground. As a result, founders suffer, and ultimately, their businesses suffer also. We can't thrive in our professional, or our personal, endeavors without the integration of heart centeredness and intellect, intuition and strategy; we must have all these things for true balance.

Like most, I didn't always subscribe to the power of integration. When I worked at the law firm, there were many people who worked harder than I did, who were more analytical and driven than me. As I continued down my career path, I thought maybe I wasn't on the right one because I lacked some of the drive and practicality of those around me. Yet at the same time, I knew I wasn't an artist, a teacher, or a super-creative type. Though I was proficient at being an attorney, and I would sometimes experience sparks of creativity, I wasn't excellent at either, and so I would often get discouraged and wonder, *Who am I?* I couldn't seem to fit nicely in either camp and was beaten down by the belief that I was going to live my life in mediocrity shoved into one box or the other. Then one afternoon, when I was struggling to find my place in the world, someone I deeply admire gave me Dan Pink's book *A Whole New Mind*. That very night, I poured myself into the inspiring text and finished reading it in only a day and a half. Pink's book was nothing short of life changing. I know this phrase sounds overly dramatic, but in this case, it was very true.

Until I received the book, I often wondered, *Am I a "left-brain" executive or a "right-brain" humanitarian? I want to be both, but society doesn't seem to embrace a blend of the two.* As I read, I was awakened to the concept of an integrated approach to life, one where we use a "whole-brain" strategy, where logic, creativity, and analytical and artistic thinking are all implemented. It was as though Pink gave me the permission I needed to embrace both sides of my personality and all of my gifts. I was invited to cultivate my innate ability to toggle back and forth between my "left-brain" qualities *and* those of my "right." I realized I had been doing this all along, never really planning for it, and that is what made my interactions with others notable. I never thought, *Ok, now I am going to shift over to my creative mind* or *Now, I am going to turn on strategic thinking.* It happened naturally within each sentence, within each breath, during every interaction. And what I came to realize is this gift is not granted to just me. We all have this ability to integrate our thoughts and actions, and if we want to reach our fullest potential, then we must invite our whole brain to activate.

Dan Pink says that it is not enough to rely on intellect alone. We need to develop empathy as well. It is the integration of logic and care that best serves others and ourselves. After reading his book, I thought, *Oh my God. I know who I am! I'm both logical and creative. I am an integration of the two. I may not be the hardest working guy in the world, but I am a smart guy who likes to work. I'm not the most artistic and creative person, but I have intuition, empathy, and a spiritual practice.* His insight gave me the confidence I needed and a foundation from which I could launch the use of my gifts in a way that made sense.

The Power of *And*

After reading, I knew one of the greatest secrets to achieving success in business and life. I knew what it could mean if people would embrace the power of *and*. I now see how lives can profoundly change for the better. I realized we don't have to choose. We don't have to give up one part of ourselves for the other. We don't have to give up passion in our businesses and lives to be prosperous. We can be loving parents *and* run successful businesses. We can have material abundance *and* be spiritually centered. This is how the universe intends for us to live.[3]

Just as I was unsure, I believe most everyone experiences uncertainty and wonders whether they are the talent or the brains. They aren't sure if they should be cranking it out at work or being in service to the softer side of their life. Perhaps you are one of them. Perhaps you struggle because you feel you have to keep one foot in each camp. Consider this: it's not about having one foot in each camp; it's about recognizing there is only one camp. Consider the phrase, *I need more work-life balance*. Really think about that for a moment. Is work not life? It's not like you leave your life to go to work. Inherent in the term *work-life balance* is the notion they are two separate things. As a result of them appearing to be separate, you need to find a way to balance them. My position is they are not separate. You have a life. In your life, you do certain things, one of them being work. There is no such thing as work-life balance; there is just balance.

The word yoga literally translates to *yoke* or *union*. Yoga is the perfect example of what it means to integrate yet, like most things, it gets put in a silo. People attend a yoga class, do their practice, roll up their mats, and step back into their perceived *other* life. They quickly forget everything they just did in class. They forget everything that the physical practice represents. They stop breathing with intention. They stop thinking about what the postures mean. They stop thinking about the fact that they just bowed at the end of class and said *namaste* as they held their hands in *anjali mudra* (commonly known as prayer). They forget that by doing this, they were saluting and honoring the divinity and light that resides in their fellow man.

With their mindset "in the other camp," they arrive at the office and forget to honor the light and divinity in others. This is *or* behavior. With the power of *and*, you can be the yogi *and* the executive. Some people will say, "So you're suggesting I do yoga in the boardroom?"

And my answer is, yes, just internally. I am not suggesting you walk around in yoga pants all the time doing Warrior II in the hallway (although I sometimes do), but you can walk into the office and carry a little bit of that experience into your meeting and into your day.

It is not unusual for me to be in board meetings and intentionally bring my yoga practice into the space. I do this by practicing *pranayama* (mindful breathing practices) or by honoring the divinity of whom I'm speaking to. Yoga is actually about so much more than what we do on the mat. The practice of yoga is about yoking the mind and the body, the spiritual and the physical, and anything we can do to bring that mindfulness to our daily life helps us integrate our lives in all ways. When I do this, I feel more calm and centered. So yes, practice yoga at work. There is no need for separation.

Separation may just be the death of us. When we don't integrate, we manage to engage in any manner of harmful behaviors. In this day and age, we ignore what our body wants and needs for the ease of processed and packaged foods. We over-train and overtax our bodies to look like an ideal that only computers can achieve. And we overwork and stress ourselves out to be more successful, all the time forgetting that we aren't happy.

This is a hard concept to grasp in the beginning, but it becomes easier with time and practice. I have struggled with it and still do from time to time. I hear people say things like, "Oh shit, I missed yoga! I've got to get that on my calendar! I've got to be better about being there!" That's force. That is intensity, and that feeling of *having* to do something is *or* based—not *and* inspired.

To begin to integrate, first start by practicing mindfulness. Catch yourself when you feel like you have to make a choice. Step back, go to that place of being aware, and ask, *Do I really have to make a choice or is something else telling me that I do?* Determine if it is one of the times that you need to turn either left or right. Ask yourself if you can integrate instead. Operate inside the bookends of extremes. I often think I need to go on a retreat in order to unplug, that I need to get away from people and technology in order to decompress. To work through this, I've chosen to make one hour every day a retreat. I go for a hike, walk through the city, or meet a buddy for lunch. I try to approach life with the power of *and*.

When someone says to me, "I'm too busy to take a vacation, I can't get out of here; business requires me to be here."

I say, "If you can't take off for two weeks and go to Europe, can you perhaps take off for three days and go to the coast?"

We have, unfortunately, lived in this world of having to make big choices and swings for a long time. The best way to tackle that is to simplify our decisions. Instead of feeling like we have to go see every one of our kids' sports games in order to be good parents, we can choose to go to one or two and while there be fully present. Instead of saying, "I'll quit smoking when I have less stress in my life," perhaps a more integrated approach is to start now by smoking three cigarettes less each day. We need to do what we can. If we can't get to yoga five days a week, we can commit to going to at least one class. Then, for ten minutes each day, we can take a break to do a few postures, and when we are waiting in line at different places, we can do so mindfully.

It will serve us well to practice patience, to breathe while we are waiting. Breathing contributes to better decision making and helps us arrive at a place of integration. Most people have very shallow breathing, and if you're one of them, commit thirty minutes each day to focusing on your breath. Do it during phone calls, while sitting with your spouse at dinner, and during business meetings. You can focus on your breathing without anyone knowing. If it would help, set alerts on your smartphone to remind you to be mindful. Perhaps remind yourself to get a glass of water every hour or to sit up straight in your chair. You will be amazed at how much better you will feel just by integrating these simple shifts. Play around and try to integrate them as best you can. Feel the change. You will likely respond so well, you'll want to do more, and not because you have to. Simplifying and being mindful will give you the freedom to integrate what has historically been a more dualistic existence.

Nature's *And* State

And is how nature works. When we are not integrating, we are not in harmony with our natural flow. We are enslaved to our ego, which is *or*. Look at the eruption of Mount St. Helens. It was a catastrophic event that cost lives, and there was devastating environmental fallout. But if you go there now, the land is flourishing. Scientists will tell you there are more wild plant species there now than ever before. The coniferous forest is coming in again, and there is more of what was supposed to be there before the eruption. This is an example of *and* in nature, yet we look at it as *or*. We look at it as black and white. We say, "Oh my God, it was awful! That volcano completely destroyed the land." Nature doesn't look at it that way.

People think of a flood as another horrible and devastating event. If you look at floods from the *and* perspective, you see they benefit the land. During a flood, river bottoms, which are incredibly nutrient rich and fertile, pour over the soil. They replenish the nutrients so plants can grow; however, it just so happens that we build structures around our rivers, so when a flood happens, we think it is devastating. To nature, it isn't.

Forest fires are another great example. We say, "Oh no, that forest fire burned thousands of acres. That's so tragic." What we don't recognize is that fire is one of nature's blessings. We see it as destruction, but nature sees it as an opportunity for creation. The fact is forests evolve in the presence of fire. They adapt to it and ultimately flourish. Forrest Hall, a physicist at NASA's Goddard Space Flight Center, explains that wildfire is an integral part of the forest ecosystem. He states that, "Fire is the mechanism by which the forest is continually regenerated." Fire burns up decaying brush on the forest floor and clears the way for new growth. Some species, such as the jack pine, rely on fire to spread their seeds. The jack pine produces resin-filled cones that are very durable. The cones remain tightly closed until a fire occurs and melts the resin. Only then can the cones pop open and the seeds distribute across the land for new growth.[4]

Fire doesn't mean destruction. Fire means opportunity. A volcanic eruption doesn't mean the world has ended; it means new life can emerge. These are prime examples of integration, yet we choose to fight against them instead of embracing this principle. I'm not suggesting we let every river flow over its banks. I'm not saying we should celebrate volcanoes, floods, and forest fires, but we can certainly start to think of things as less black and white when we consider the way nature works.

Consider the periodic table of elements. Elements are the building blocks of life and certain ones sync up beautifully. When they come together, they form chemical bonds. These bonds, such as hydrogen and oxygen, create things like water. Conversely, we have plutonium and uranium. If you take those two and try to force them together, the result is nuclear fusion. We end up with a massive catastrophe of radiation and death. This is true for our lives as well. Unfortunately, we spend a lot of our time trying to bang plutonium and uranium together, and we are surprised when there is a nuclear reaction. Instead, we should be looking at our lives and saying, "I embrace *and*. I embrace what is flowing and recognize where I have strong chemical bonds." We should also look at our lives and examine where things aren't coming together, where they are not flowing. It's likely those things are occurring from an *or* place, and it may be best to move on before there is an explosion.

People who believe you should have your cake but not eat it are living in tyranny. That kind of thinking is unnatural. People have said to me, "You can't be in the business community and smoke pot." They think that doing so somehow means I am lazy and won't be respected. They have implied that if I smoke marijuana once in a while, I won't be as effective in business because my head will be in the clouds. I say that is absurd. Now, I agree that perhaps it's not the best idea to smoke weed all day, but for someone to give me, or any professional, shit for smoking a joint on the weekend while at home watching a movie is ridiculous. They are subscribing to *or* thinking and are limiting their joy. Little by little, this thinking is changing. I am an agent of that change. I like disruptive companies and brands that are moving from a place of *or* to one of *and*. I support those who are changing the world in the face of adversity.

So I ask you: Do you have a good relationship with your children *and* give your best at work? Does your work support your prosperity *and* feed your soul? Are you connected with your spouse *and* yourself in an authentic and loving way? If not, take a step back and look at where you are not integrating. Choose to have it all. Choose to create safety and security while at the same time embracing equal amounts of spirituality, culture, art, relationships, and self-love. Weave the left and the right—and never apologize for being both the executive and the man or woman who smokes pot once in a while.

6

TRUST AND SURRENDER:
WELCOMING THE UNKNOWN

"The most visible creators I know of are those artists whose
medium is life itself . . . They are the artists of being alive."

—**J. Stone**

To the typical "left-brain" thinker, my wife, Heather, would not be
considered the type to build, let alone sell, a successful business.
She does not have an advanced business degree, and she doesn't
access her analytical, business side as much as she does her creative side. When she began to develop Oregon Chai, I still believed
the path to abundance was one of hard work, of being smarter,
faster, or better, so I was, shamelessly, one of the people who didn't
believe in her. Heather proved all of us nonbelievers wrong. She
created Oregon Chai from the perspective of a pure mind filled with
wonder. She was impervious to the word *can't*. She was going to
succeed at building her business, and she knew her vision to be absolutely true.

Heather is one of my greatest teachers when it comes to the principles of trust and surrender. At first, I thought she was out of her
damn mind when the spark ignited within her and she said to me

one day, "I want to start a chai company, David." I was immediately annoyed. At the time, we had student loans piling up, I was just finishing law school and did not yet have a job, she didn't have a job, and we needed to start looking for work and saving for a house. So when it sounded like she wanted to have a hobby that would look something like owning a company, I told her it wasn't happening. I flat out did not support her. She ignored me.

It's important to note this occurred about one year prior to my getting a job at the law firm and two years prior to the night my eyes fell on the Preparation H. When Heather began brewing chai, I was not living my dharma. I was still stuck in the abyss, and so any spark of ingenuity that did not fit into my known world of possibility was out of the question. Thinking back on it now, I shudder to consider that, had she listened to me, we may not have experienced the great fortune we did nor would we have enhanced the lives of millions of consumers worldwide with her tasty brew.

I couldn't stop Heather, but I did not back off on making snide remarks or patronizing and undermining her. I would say things like, "Why don't you do what the rest of the world does and use your degree to get a job?" Enraged, sometimes I would plead with her to stop spending the little income we had on cinnamon, clove, honey, and milk. She would just tune me out and carry on. After about a year of this, I got the job from hell. You can imagine how this escalated my anger and resentment of her pursuit. The more I hated life because of the bottomless chasm I lived in during the day, the more I resented her and her sweet, hot tea when I'd get home at night. There were countless days when I would walk through the door at 10 PM feeling like ulcers were bleeding right out of me, ridden with exhaustion, and completely drained of every ounce of life. Heather would start complaining about how a batch of chai didn't work out that day or that the tea she was trying to source went up in price. I'm not sure why or how she would put up with me when a typical response to that would sound something like, "I'm fucking exhausted, Heather. I've been busting my ass all day billing hours and you're here telling me how your little tea idea isn't tracking? Fuck! This is not what we're supposed to be doing right now. We're both supposed to be working like everyone else—going to the office, doing the grind, so we can live the American dream!"

She would respond sweetly, still focused on her hope and intention, saying, "I don't believe that, David. The people trying this love it, and they want more. I can't stop. I won't stop."

Others who were living in their abyss also thought she was crazy. They would ask about her business plan, her addressable market size, her competitors, her P&L, and five-year strategy. She would respond by telling them she didn't know, but she did know that people everywhere were going to think chai was amazing. She visualized people drinking her product and enjoying it in the same way she did. She visualized them experiencing nirvana by way of a creamy beverage infused with vanilla, cinnamon, ginger, and honey. It was a heart-centered birthing of a product that stemmed from her commitment to brewing the perfect cup. It was never about how much money it was going to make or what our margins would be. She always stayed focused on the passion.

We all have the drive to share our gifts, despite our egos telling us it is safer to remain hidden in the familiar comfort zone of an average life. We are all made of cosmic elements that make us destined to mature and transform. The hero archetype lives within all of us, and it brings with it the potential power to shine and surpass our wildest dreams. This innate birthright to become a source of light in our world is possible for everyone. It is manifested in our lives, sometimes when we do not even expect it, in places such as our businesses. As Steve Jobs said, "Your work is going to fill a large part of your life, and the only way to be truly satisfied is to do what you believe is great work. The only way to do great work is to love what you do. If you haven't found it yet, keep looking. Don't settle. As with all matters of the heart, you'll know when you find it."[1] Discovering our purpose, loving what we do, and then going out and sharing our gifts with others is what will heal the world.

Heather was in a place of trust and surrender, in a place of living her bliss and sharing her gift with the world. She was operating from her heart and staying true to her passion despite it looking completely impractical and like a waste of time and money to me. I am not proud of those first two years, but I am grateful for her being one of my greatest teachers. Trust and manifestation have always come so easily to her, and by her example, I learned to implement these tools in my life.

Dave Dahl of Dave's Killer Bread has a truly remarkable journey as well. Dave spent fifteen years in the federal penitentiary as a felon. For many years leading up to his conviction and throughout his time behind bars, especially toward the latter part of his third stint in prison, Dave started to turn his life around. He began to embrace a healthy diet and the idea of nourishing himself from within.

When he was released from prison, he left with the idea for Dave's Killer Bread, a different way of making and sharing this universal staple. His family had a small bread business in Oregon, and to create the product, he didn't conduct consumer research. He didn't hire a fancy consulting firm. He did nothing more than proceed with his heart, soul, and vision leading the way. From his simple belief of possibility, he was able to get his brother, father, and nephew to listen to his idea. After a great deal of convincing and a bit of hesitation, they gave him a chance, and he birthed a company that exceeds fifty million dollars in revenue every year. It was less than five years ago that Dave himself was setting up a booth every Saturday at the Portland State farmer's market, inviting people to try his product.

After a few years of people embracing his story and bread, he sought support to take his business to the next level. He enrolled consultants to support him on his journey by bringing in the necessary financial partners and by developing a clear strategy for expansion.

He trusted and surrendered. He welcomed the guidance, so he could take his vision, heart, and soul and marry them with sound business practices. As a result, Dave's Killer Bread is rolling out from the Pacific Northwest to California and Arizona and will eventually sweep the entire nation. To this day, Dave routinely tells others that the money flowing in just means he can deliver more nourishing and killer bread into more mouths. All he wants is to make the most kickass bread the world has ever tasted. If he can help kids and adults eat better sandwiches and ensure more tasty and nourishing toast in the morning, then he has done something right in the world. To him, it is nothing more than that.

Not only is Dave's story about trust and surrender, but it is also a story of redemption that defies all traditional belief systems with respect to business. Yes, he was a felon. Yes, he burglarized homes. Yes, he did meth. Yes, he was a broken spirit for a long time—*and* he is a wonderful, humble, spiritual, and amazing man. He is a man whose life is committed to feeding wholesome bread to millions of people. His is also a story of *and*.

Surrender to Transform

This idea of trust and surrender is very pure, and it is necessary to embrace during our transformation if we wish to reach our defining moment. When we trust, the activities of our lives occur with greater ease. They don't occur through force or from beating our heads against the wall. They don't come from working brutally long hours or from being faster, smarter, more manipulative, or even just more able than the other guy. Great things happen through recognizing we can set an intention, plant it in fertile soil, nurture it with trust, and it will sprout and grow. Oregon Chai, yogitoes, Dave's Killer Bread, and countless other businesses illustrate this process in action. They demonstrate that trust and surrender, when applied with action, create success.

To check and see whether or not you are really surrendering, see how you feel in your body and evaluate your feelings in reference to recent events. If you feel tight or if your heart is racing, then you are probably not sharing the burdens of your life with the divine. You are likely carrying too much responsibility. At this point in my life, I am able to read my body's responses pretty well. I am quick to realize if I am functioning from a place of surrender versus struggle. Like you, I am human, so I do not always adhere to this tool perfectly. In fact, I often don't, but I still know what is right, and if I choose to make a decision otherwise and force a situation that I know is maybe not best for me, I do it with complete awareness.

A sign that you are operating from a place of trust and surrender is that time is no longer linear—there is no difference between five minutes or five hours—because you are so caught up in the moment, so caught up in the task or project you are working on that you no longer even mark time. It is when everything happens with ease and you see great results.

If you don't see results, are not having fun, and time drags on, then you are likely not on the right path. In those times, I would suggest you step back and take a look at the situation with a broader lens. Try to reconfigure by adjusting the composition. Reset your focus and then ask:

- Am I having fun?
- Am I seeing results?
- Am I feeling joyous?

If your answer is no to any of those, stop what you are doing and move on.

Trust and surrender are two of the more difficult principles to embrace because it is engrained in our minds that work is toil, work is hard, and life is hard. We're conditioned to believe that, if you want to be wealthy and have abundance, you have to sacrifice a lot; that to be successful, insomnia is a fact of life; and that caffeine and Preparation H are acceptable prescriptions for dulling the pain. You expect your life will not be filled with happiness, ease, and flow. I struggle with the idea that life *should* be filled with happiness to this day. There are times I will take off from the office in the middle of the afternoon to go for a long run in the Portland hills. I'll be surrounded by the most picturesque nature scene, breathing in rich air, yet amidst the blissful experience, I will be ridden with anxiety. I'll think, *I shouldn't be doing this. I have a business to run. People are counting on me. Oh shit, I didn't bring my phone with me on my run! What if someone is trying to get ahold of me?* In those moments, I have to consciously slow my breathing and remind myself that a run in the park is exactly what I should be doing. We all need to be feeding and nurturing ourselves.

When enough people start to trust and come to know that surrender is not an action of weakness but a willingness to be led by the divine, magic will happen in all of our lives. It is then the world can transform. It's like when Glinda the Good Witch said to Dorothy, "All you needed to do was click your heels together three times and you could have returned to Kansas. You've always had the power within you."[2] We are no different. Our divinity is internal. It is within us. We all carry with us *ruach*, the breath of God, the source energy, our shared divinity, or whatever label you wish to give it. We just need to tap into that truth. When we arrive at a place of trust, surrender to something bigger than ourselves, and choose to live in flow, miracles can happen.

The more of us who put energy into healthy transformation and build on these thoughts and feelings together, the more powerful the result. Three different studies done between 1983–1995—two studies done in the United States and one in Holland—divided approximately 7,000 meditators into groups and had them meditate on nonviolence for periods lasting from eight to eleven days. The effects were studied using terrorism data collected independently by the Rand Corporation, the renowned California think tank. The study reports that five days after the assemblies started, terrorist activities in the world calmed down. It also found that warfare due to national and international conflicts decreased by approximately 30 percent. Assessment of the effects on warfare came from reports appearing in the *New York Times* and *London Times*.[3]

In the eight limbs of yoga, one of the *niyamas* (self-restraints) is *ishvara pranidhana*. One interpretation of this observance is "surrender to a supreme source"—a force greater than ourselves. By adhering to this principle, we shift our perspective from one of "I," which is egocentric, separates us from source, and limits our potential, to one of divine power. *Ishvara pranidhana* reminds us we are connected with the divine. Patanjali tells us that surrender is not something we do when we are ready to give up. Rather, we are to surrender in all activities of our lives—to trust in divine will, to trust in divine timing. And that from that place, we will be supported on our path because we will be in alignment with our True Self.

Most people believe that to succeed in business, bulldog-like persistence is needed. While it is true that perseverance is necessary and often rewarded, there are times when trusting and surrendering to the universe can accomplish just as much if not more. For example, say you have had several meetings with a potential client, and you are especially eager to sign a service contract with them. Your initial reaction may be to call and email them until you get that agreement signed. But such relentless persistence can be a turn-off and may cause you to lose their business. In this particular case, if you had simply been patient and trusted that they would sign the contract when they were ready, not only would you have gained the new client, but you also would have gained their respect and appreciation for your patience with the process.

Unfortunately, many struggle with this because they equate surrender with weakness. They feel someone else is going to dominate or own them if they let go and trust. In reality, this couldn't be further from the truth. Take a look at the aikido master. He surrenders. That is all he does to beat his opponent. And the master is not weak. He surrenders the need to control and in doing so has complete control. If you were to watch a match, you'd see that when someone attacks, the master will simply step out of the way, and the person tumbles and falls—or the master will use the energy, the inertia of the attacker's blow, to bring him down. When you surrender to those things you don't need to control or that you can't control, an exuberant amount of energy is freed up to be used in more useful ways.

Some of the greatest athletes demonstrate surrender in their sport. Take Wayne Gretzky for example, who is arguably the greatest hockey player of all time. Though he gives the game his all, he is fluid and in flow on the ice. He makes an undeniably difficult and strategic game look effortless. It's the same when the dancer and the dance merge—or when the poet and the poem become one. When you choose to surrender, you become aligned with the source, the universe. When you do all you can to follow your instincts and then turn them over, the surrendering makes miracles happen. Buddha reminds us that, if you surrender the ego, if you surrender yourself, you come into harmony with universal law and everything starts happening on its own.

We have all experienced really bad days, months, or even years as a result of forced action. During those periods, it is not unusual to feel like we need to fix ourselves, like if we did more therapy, exercised more, or prayed more, we'd pull through, we'd get back on our feet again. But what often happens when we force ourselves is that we get worse—depression deepens, anxiety increases. Why? Because we are trying too hard. We are trying to control something that we are not meant to control. If we can just surrender to the universe, our lives will turn around—maybe not immediately, but we will see gradual shifts toward feeling whole again.

We have all been in the situation where we're late for an appointment and feeling completely frantic. The internal dialogue of, *I'm lost, I'm late*, makes the drive even worse. Every green light turns red. We take a wrong turn. The train shows up. Our hearts race and we soak our shirts in sweat. That one stressful drive ruins our entire days. Whereas if we can just take a breath and say, *Okay, the sky is blue today and I'm heading to a meeting. It's not like I am rushing to the hospital to open up someone's head to repair their brain.*

Then we need to give ourselves a little love, knowing people will understand. Lights will turn green, traffic will recede, and we will arrive nearly on time. The next time this or something like it happens to you, think of Luke Skywalker when the Death Star is closing in on the rebel base. He's freaking out because his GPS isn't working and then he hears Obi-Wan Kenobi say, "Use the Force, Luke."[4] Obi-Wan is basically saying, *Chill out, Luke. Just breathe and trust.*

And he does. He takes the goggles from his eyes, his energy shifts, he takes a deep breath, and is like, *I got this.*

7

CO-CREATION AND THE POWER OF MANIFESTATION:
An Infinite Field of Possibilities

"The ones who are crazy enough to think that they can change the world, are the ones who do."

—Steve Jobs

I have always believed in the power of manifestation. This tool has been available to me ever since I was a young boy. In the introduction, I talk about how, in order to manifest peace in my crappy home environment, I would imagine filling the room with gold light. The light would become so bright in my mind and the quarrels and tension would subside.

Later in life, I was able to use this tool of manifestation as well. One summer in high school, I wanted to work outdoors, instead of working inside at a fast-food chain or bowling alley. I visualized myself in nature, working autonomously. That spark of desire led me to the idea of going door-to-door to each homeowner and offering to stencil yellow street numbers on the front curb of each house. Neighbors loved the service, and I made five dollars per job, significantly more than my friends who worked for minimum wage. I just needed to set the intention and it became reality.

This ability to manifest and co-create is often exemplified in children. My son, Sawyer, not unlike a lot of kids, has always been a very intuitive child. One Saturday afternoon when he was five years old, we were in the yard together. It was a warm and sunny day, and I was doing yard work while he played. Sawyer had an affinity for reptiles, and had several snakes and lizards that he kept in the house and meticulously cared for at the time. On this particular day, he was hell-bent on finding another to add to his collection. He came running over and asked, "Hey, Dad, will you help me find a snake?" I was in a state of mind where looking for a snake felt like a burden. I wanted to hurry up and get my yard work done so I could check other things off my list like a hike, a trip to the store, and some downtime with an ice-cold beer.

As a result of wanting to stick to my to-do list, I responded dickishly, telling him I was too busy. Mind you, this was not one of my proudest moments. He kept at me seven or eight more times, and I finally said, "I'm not going to look for a snake with you, Sawyer. I'm busy right now and need to get this yard work done. I've lived here thirteen years and worked countless hours in the yard, and I have never seen a snake. But if you want to go look for a snake, go look for a snake." With wanderlust and complete innocence in his eyes, he ran off into the yard. Almost immediately, I was taken aback by my reaction and felt like an asshole. His innocent desire to find a snake and my reaction to him suddenly awoke in me a keen awareness of the moment. I felt awful about my reaction.

This checking in with myself took all of thirty seconds, and before I was done, Sawyer shouted, "Hey, Dad, look!" I turned around and there he was, holding a snake.

Every hair on my body stood up, my eyes filled with tears, I couldn't breathe, and I was barely able to stammer out, "Where did you . . . how did you . . . ?"

He said, "I just thought to myself, if I were a snake, where would I be? Then I put my mind in the mind of the snake. Then I was the snake, slithering through the grass. Then I thought, since I am the snake, I know where I am. Then I just reached my hand down into the grass by the shed, and I pulled me out of the grass."

Needless to say, I was stunned. I had just witnessed co-creation with the divine. It was profound and life altering, as I was reminded we all have that power to manifest, all the time, every day, every second—but we lose it through growing up with social conditioning. When you are an innocent child, before being beaten down by people telling you not to trust, surrender, or manifest, all things are possible. You don't think twice about raising up your wishes and trusting wholeheartedly they will come to be.

The moment my son visualized becoming a snake and then pulled one from the grass was a turning point in my life. My belief in manifestation and the concept of co-creation was strengthened. I integrate these two principles into my life every day. Sometimes I call on them for simple things, such as front-row parking or for a red light to turn green. Other manifestations are more significant.

One time, I was catching the train at Union Station to travel from Portland to Seattle. My morning meetings had backed up, and I had to rush there mere minutes before departure. When I pulled into the roundabout, I visualized leaving my car in the drive, running into the station, and leaping onto the train car just as it was pulling away. That vision became reality; the train literally pulled away just as my foot made contact with it. When in my seat, I called Heather to let her know I had abandoned my car in the no-stopping, no-waiting zone of the station. I let her know the keys were in the ignition and asked if she could please take a cab to pick it up.

She agreed but was certain she'd find the car missing, either having been impounded or towed. In her mind, the only other realistic possibility was that she would find it in front with a wheel boot or a big fat ticket. I knew otherwise. I was certain it would be untouched, just where I left it. And it was. Heather was astounded because of the unlikeliness of it—but she was not surprised by my ability to manifest a situation that would work beautifully to support my need at the time.

The opportunities made possible by manifestation are endless. All you need is belief in the infinite power of the collective unconscious, an intention, and the ability to surrender. It is this special cocktail of tools that makes all desires reality. When you trust and surrender, you turn your desires over to the universe for manifestation. Doing so requires you be flexible with the outcome. It means you step away and let the cosmos take care of the details, like me wanting to work outside that summer—I didn't know what I would be doing; I just knew I wanted to be outside. The universe worked out all the particulars. My son didn't know where the snake was. He just knew if he could visualize becoming a snake, he'd know where to look in order to pluck one from the grass. Heather didn't know how she was going to share chai with the world; she just knew people everywhere would love it once it filled their mug. We will undoubtedly experience more joy and move closer to our defining moment if we become aware of the power of this energy and believe manifestations are occurring all the time.

A man told me a story recently that beautifully illustrates the power of manifestation. After scouring the job market for quite a long time, his son finally found a job but did not have transportation to get there. Neither the man nor his son had money to buy a car. With his first day fast approaching, the only foreseeable solution was for the man to drive his son to work every day, greatly inconveniencing himself. This was going to be draining on both of them, so the dad set an intention to get a car. He had no idea how it was going to be possible; he just trusted God would support him in making it so.

Within a few days of his son accepting the job, the father visited a nearby market. As he left the store, he happened to take note of a car at the edge of the parking lot, sitting alone. Following his instincts, he walked over to the vehicle and noted its expired plates. He went back into the market to ask if anyone knew about the vehicle, something that even to him seemed rather absurd, considering people drive with expired plates all the time. Nevertheless, he was inspired to do so.

The manager said it had been sitting there for quite a while but didn't have any recommendations for the man. Yet again, he went with his gut and contacted the police department, who directed him to the parking lot owners. They were well aware of the abandoned car. The owner had passed away, and for months, the car had sat there unclaimed. They had intended to tow it within the next forty-eight hours so were delighted to grant this man permission to remove it from their lot. Being that it was a much older model of car, he had no trouble getting keys made, and when he went to the DMV for licensing, he was surprised to experience effortless registration. This man was gifted a car for his son by the universe—and it was made possible by him being tuned in to manifestation; by him going with the flow and following his impulses, one leading to the next, his wish for a car was granted. When we desire something or set an intention and then follow the flow of our impulses, we co-create with the universe and the potentiality of achieving our desires increases.

Tuning In

Unlike the man in this story, we are frequently not tuned in to our synchronicities and manifestations. We are usually unaware of them first being constructed in our subconscious. From there, by way of dreams, daydreams, or unconscious thought, they are sent out into the universe. As Deepak Chopra points out, all of us are multitasking all the time, navigating the four levels of ourselves—being, feeling, thinking, and doing. Our feelings and our thoughts, both conscious and subconscious, become things and experiences. As they co-create with and are delivered into the universe, they quite literally shape our lives. Remember, as Michael Bernard Beckwith points out in *The Secret*,

"What you are thinking now is creating your future life. You create your life with your thoughts . . . , what you think about the most or focus on the most is what will appear as your life."[1] Depending on our thoughts and beliefs, we can manifest either the positive or the negative. If you function from a place of negativity, you will co-create more of the same. If your intentions are masked by fear, what you manifest in the physical plane may not serve your basic needs of experiencing joy and love. Just like what happens if we don't accept our shadow selves, if we put energy or thought into what we don't want, we will get more of it!

Think about the accumulation of debt. When you fear having more bills, a walk to the mailbox may trigger a need for Xanax. When you have constant concern for running late, every stoplight on your route is a standing red. Even two such disparate historical figures as Carl Jung and Henry Ford are both said to have commented on this; Carl Jung is widely quoted as saying, "What you resist persists," and Henry Ford is said to have put it, "Whether you think you can or can't, you're right." This goes for what you think consciously *and* unconsciously. So when you have moments of worry and concern, stop, breathe, and consciously choose to have a positive thought to counteract the negative. If you are late, instead of fanning the flaming thoughts of running behind, take a breath. Consider that you have no control over traffic lights and other drivers, and so getting upset and worrying does not have the possibility of a positive outcome. All you can do is relax, surrender to the traffic, and trust you will arrive when the universe intends. In these small ways, you can shift your thinking from being antagonistic to being more life affirming, and when you do, you will attract more of what you want, rather than what you don't want.

There is an old tale accepted as one of the many teachings of Sri Ramakrishna Paramahamsa Deva, passed down through the generations that illustrates the concept of co-creation so simply. It tells the story of the *Kalpataru* tree, which in Sanskrit, is translated to mean "wish-fulfilling tree." In Indian mythology, the tree sym-bolically represents the mind's power of manifestation. In the tale, a man, exhausted from his travels, stumbles into a paradise and rests beneath a *Kalpataru* tree. He does not know that if you sit beneath the tree, whatever you desire will be granted. Since, in Vedic teach-ings, thoughts become things, whatever thoughts this man had while sitting under the tree would come to be. The tired man fell asleep and, when he woke hungry, said, "I am so hungry. I wish I had some food."

Food appeared instantly, just floating in the air, and the man ate in such haste that he didn't put any thought into where the food had come from. Once he had eaten all the food, another thought came to mind: *If only I had something to drink.* Right then, wine appeared. While drinking the wine, he started wondering what was going on. *There must be some ghosts around playing tricks with me.* Then, fero-cious ghosts appeared, scaring the man. He began to tremble and another thought arose.

Now I am sure to be killed. These ghosts are going to kill me. And he was killed.

This parable is an ancient one with many different versions, but regardless of the version, it always bears the same message: our minds are our wish-fulfilling trees, and whatever we think, believe in, and direct our attention to, the universe will deliver on sooner or later—and sometimes even instantly.

An actualized desire is not always an obvious one. Being flexi-ble with the outcome and realizing when our positive intentions are being manifested takes trust and surrender. It also takes practice. The more we work on tapping into our manifestations in the moment, the more we will become adept at doing so—and manifesting joy will eventually become effortless.

When Sawyer found the snake, it wasn't until I shouted at him that I became aware of my to-do list mindset—that's because, for us humans, *not* living in the moment can also be effortless. But not living in the moment robs us of our highest potential. We are meant to live in the present, connected to our surroundings and tuned in to our experience. I could have been in a much better place that day if I had chosen to appreciate being one with nature, the beautiful flowers in my yard, and my precious child. I could have more fully participated in his joy and his moment of manifestation, and as a result, would have felt better about myself and been more connected with my son.

There is a story about a man trapped on top of his house during a flood with the water swiftly rising. As the man sits on his roof, scared of being swept away, he cries out to God, "God, please deliver me." A few moments later, a neighbor arrives with his boat, but the man says, "No thank you. God is going to save me."

An hour later, the water is up to the gutters. A volunteer rescue person comes by on his yellow raft. "Hey, climb down and jump in the raft!" he yells. But the man on top of his house refuses to go.

"God is going to deliver me," he replies. Another hour passes, and now the water is halfway up the roof. The man is on top of his chimney, terrified and looking down at his impending death.

Just then, a volunteer with the Red Cross shows up in a canoe and offers to take the man to safety. And yet again he refuses, saying, "No, God is going to save me." A couple hours pass, the water sweeps over the top of the house, and the man is carried away by the current and drowns. When he gets to heaven, he meets God and says, "I thought you were going to deliver me."

God looks at the man and says, "I did all I could. I sent a boat, an inflatable raft, and a canoe, but you refused each one."

In some cases, like the man on the roof, having awareness that you just co-created an event can spare your life. At the very least, it can help you experience joy in the present moment. Tuning in to manifestations occurring in the now can also help you shape your reality. Each time you realize the power that co-created your desire, you set an intention for the next manifestation and the next, and so on.

Controlling Your Subconscious

Just as important as tapping into our moments of manifestation is the practice of having control over our subconscious. At any time, we can shift our internal dialogue. As we begin to integrate and practice the principles of manifestation, our subconscious will begin to rewire. Our entire being will transform. When we know this on an experiential level, we spontaneously realize that we have choices and that we can exercise these choices. What is most detrimental to our ability to manifest is a loss of trust. When we fail to turn our heart-centered desires over to the divine, the actualization of our highest potential is put at risk.

Believing in co-creation means we believe in the power of manifesting with the support of the universe. When our desires are heart centered and in the spirit of service, our manifestations help the world become a better place. We are always looked after when we commit to being of service. Through heeding our unique callings, we enroll the universe in blessing us with goodness. It is through our sacred contract with the divine that we will have enough prosperity to get our work into the world in a meaningful way and live a life of abundance. To co-create and manifest, we need to align our soul's desires with the spirit of our higher purpose.

Ancient masters refer to the flow of creation, or manifestation, as *bhukti* (meaning "enjoyment"). On this path, creativity originates in the plane of pure awareness, also known as the collective unconscious. The creative energy enters your being in the form of an idea or thought, and is then shaped and molded until it can shift into action and words. Once it has enough energetic density, you see the creativity manifest in the world. You will see this happen more in your life when you focus attention on your dharma.

We have an incredible opportunity to shift our success in business for the better. Financial abundance, rich relationships, and longevity are all within arm's reach when we use co-creation and manifestation.

An inspiring business example of the power of manifestation is the story of Jay Graves, founder of Bike Gallery. For thirty years, he built an iconic Portland-based bicycle service and retail brand. He has always been deeply involved in the community and committed to building lasting relationships. To be of service in the world and to provide customers the highest quality experience possible, Jay poured genuine care and attention into his brand, products, and services. He also passionately fostered and supported his staff, empowering them to reach their highest potential. After three decades of building his business, Jay began to consider moving on to other projects and interests. He started to focus on an exit strategy. He consciously, and subconsciously, delivered his desire into the universe without any preconceived ideas of what it should look like. One afternoon, while meeting with his financial planner, he shared this desire, and his planner suggested a team of advisors that could possibly help him with an exit that would not compromise his brand integrity.

Jay met with the advisors and explained to them the values he would not allow to be compromised by the sale. It was imperative that whoever purchased Bike Gallery preserve brand integrity and employee empowerment, support of the community, and unsurpassed customer service. Not only did the advisors deeply understand and respect Jay's desire for keeping these values intact, but they also knew the right buyers would be one of Jay's principle managers and Mike Olson of Trek Bicycles. Both shared the same values as Jay, and after Jay was introduced to Mike, the sale of Bike Gallery closed in just eighty-three days. Jay manifested the exit, only truly aiming to in no way compromise the principles he wanted Bike Gallery to stay true to, and the transition was a smooth, positive one for all involved.

Wherever you are on your personal and professional journey, recognizing the sacred force and empowerment within you honors the bountifulness of the universe.

8

LIVING IN FLOW:
Balancing Humility and Empowerment

"The reason why many are still troubled, still seeking,
still making little forward progress is because they haven't yet
come to the end of themselves. We're still trying to give orders,
and interfering with God's work within us."

—A. W. Tozer

Much like we have been taught that we must focus on developing our logical, analytical mind to succeed and have therefore lived most of our lives in the tyranny of *or*, we have also been instructed to believe success means doing it all ourselves. Our egos tell us we must be in control and charge forward at all costs. They tell us that to surrender means we are weak and that giving up or shifting gears will leave us powerless. Conversely, science, nature, religion, and myth all show that when you hoard control, you cut yourself off from universal flow and ultimately stagnate. You toil beyond what is necessary and cease to be in alignment with your journey. Even hanging on to your own guilt and not practicing forgiveness of yourself and others is hoarding and egocentric.

A high vibration of *prana*, life force, expands health in the universe, whereas a decrease in *prana* contributes to lack, illness, depression, and universal suffering. When you find yourself in *prana*-decreasing circumstances, such as engaging in negative mind chatter, gossip, or not speaking the truth, try a quick exercise to snap yourself out of it. Take a deep breath and hold it until it becomes uncomfortable. It will not take long for your body to enter a state of panic, and you'll have no choice but to exhale. This exercise will serve to remind you that so much of how we operate in our lives is like an inhale needing to be released. It will drive home the idea that you are not in flow.

So often, we hang on to memories, habits, and programming that no longer serve us, and like in that breath, we inflict pain when we hold on for too long. We do this because the breath originally served us well through its oxygenating, life-affirming qualities, but very quickly, it is used up and needs be let go of. In just seconds, it shifts from life sustaining to life threatening.

There is a tale of two monks who were making a pilgrimage to pay reverence to a great saint. While on their journey, they traveled along a river. There, they met a beautiful young woman—a material creature who was dressed in fine clothing and donned a fashionable hairstyle. She wanted to cross the river but was afraid of the current and feared ruining her expensive clothes. She asked the two monks if they would be willing to carry her across to the other side. The younger and more dogmatic of the two was offended and shunned the idea. The older monk didn't hesitate. He swept up the beautiful woman and carried her across the river. She thanked him and went on her way. The monks resumed their walk, the older one feeling in flow and aligned, taking in the beauty of the countryside. The younger monk was stewing in his thoughts, brooding over what had just occurred. He could no longer hold back his disgust and burst out, "Brother, we are taught to avoid contact with women, and there you were, not just touching a woman, but carrying her on your shoulders!"

The older and wiser monk looked at the younger with a loving smile and said, "Brother, I set her down on the other side of the river. Why are you still carrying her?"

This story beautifully illustrates how we can unconsciously carry burdens that do not serve us. Like after the breath has completed its intended task, when we let go—when we exhale—we make room for another rich inhale, another opportunity. We say to the universe, "I have created space for more life-affirming experiences." It is these individual inhales, these new opportunities in life, that create our journey. This is living in flow.

Straining and striving are counterproductive. To be masters of our own lives, we should live in accordance with *wu wei*, which in English means "non-action." High-achieving workaholic types say this is an eloquent way to describe laziness, but there is a better inter-pretation. Non-action means to be so in touch with our environment, with the will of the divine, and with the people in our lives that our actions flow naturally. They are not forced, controlled, or microman-aged. When we exhibit *wu wei*, we simply go with the flow of things. If we can learn to relax and trust, our lives will flow just as the tides rise and flowers bloom. Our will to let go will allow for nothing but total alignment and ease.

There is a profound geographical representation of *wu wei* found in the Middle East: the River Jordan, which flows into Israel and feeds two seas. The first sea is so clean and beautiful it regularly attracts kids and families to picnic there. Birds and fish thrive in and near the water. Along its banks, plants flourish and the water sparkles like diamonds in contrast to the outlying stark land. The second sea, despite being fed by the same river, is completely barren. There are no fish, no trees, no plankton, no families picnicking on the banks, no abundance, and no diamond-like shimmer. Curiously, there is only one differentiating factor between the two bodies of water. For every ounce of water that flows into the first sea, the Sea of Galilee, an ounce of water is let out. Water flows through, and as a result, there is abundance. The second sea, aptly named the Dead Sea, hoards the River Jordan. It does not release an ounce of her. There is no outlet. There is no flow. Like the ego, it holds on and does not want to give. It wants to own it all, and in that sea, you have death.

Growing up in the Midwest in a home that espoused the "work hard and toil" ideology, I believed this was the correct way to live until finally heeding my impulses to leave the known world and head west. It was by witnessing Heather's birthing of Oregon Chai that I began to see you could achieve much better results without having to kill yourself. As I welcomed this new way of thinking, my initial feeling was that it couldn't be right. As I began to play with the concept of flow, I felt guilty. Childhood programming dominated my psyche. It had me believe that manifesting dreams or being able to earn money quickly was a result of luck or manipulation. Yet, as I continued to practice loosening the reigns, it became clearer that I wasn't the one controlling the outcome. I realized you can choose to work your butt off and take little wins and losses and only end up at about neutral, or you can subscribe to the concept of *wu wei* and end up with a positive every time.

Accepting Our Roles as Co-Creators

As important as a take-charge attitude can be, it is still only half the equation. We can accomplish so much more if we allow the universe to work its magic. You see, our view of possibility is limited by our temporal knowledge, but the divine knows all things and knows what needs to take place, what ears it needs to whisper in, and which eyes need to be opened in order for our desired results to be actualized.

Hafiz, the beloved Sufi poet, wrote, "I am a hole in a flute that Christ's breath moves through . . . Listen to this music."[1] The ego only hears arrogance in these poetic words. The ego believes Hafiz is claiming divine authority, which couldn't be further from the truth. Hafiz is not saying he is the flute; he's just saying he is a *hole* in the flute through which divine breath can flow. He is illustrating the truth that we are all vessels for downloading the universe's energy through the analogy of the flute. This energy flows into us, takes shape from our unique molding, and then flows through, carrying our gifts into the world. It is a beautiful illustration of the balance between doing and not doing, of humility and empowerment. In my life, when I have been in flow and living *wu wei*, synchronicities abound, life is easy, I see results, and I have fun.

When we hold tight, when we feel like it is us doing, rather than us co-creating, life is hard work. But when we recognize there is something else helping us along, life feels like running with a strong wind at our back. Yes, we have to tie on our shoes, head out the door, and move our bodies, but with a strong wind at our back, the exertion feels more effortless. Sometimes we set out on the run, setting our course in the direction we think we should be going, only to encounter a resistant wind at our face, and it doesn't matter how fit we are; the run will be harder. Yet when we implement the principle of letting go, we say we are willing to have the wind direct us, that we are open to changing the direction in which we think we should be traveling. Maybe we go left this time, or maybe we go right. And maybe we arrive at our destination via a whole new way, but at least we have the support of the wind to carry us—and at least we do still arrive.

If you aren't feeling the ease of your pursuit, turn around, shift direction, and the wind will be there to carry you. In your life and business, learn to make adjustments when you feel like you are beating a dead horse. If you are struggling, step back and listen to that centered part of you, your soul. Ask what you can do to reformat or realign. Then listen. The answer may be as simple as turning around or repositioning yourself. Sometimes the answer will be to stop what you are doing altogether and try something else.

If you pay attention, you will always know if you're living in *wu wei*. You will see results; what you are pursuing will be easier than you thought. You'll tend to have fun, and time will cease to be linear.

If you find yourself saying, "Wow, it's already three 'o clock? Seems like I just got into the office." You are likely in flow. You are in the zone. Alternatively, if you just can't seem to get going or can't figure something out after multiple attempts, you may need to take a look at where you are putting your energy. If you are always feeling like you're stuck in a rut, like everything is going wrong, and there are red lights at every intersection, you are likely not accepting your role as co-creator with the universe.

Just like plutonium and uranium, you can bang them together all you want, but force will only result in explosion. Your body and emotions send you alerts when you are trying to force chemical bonds. If you feel calm, healthy, happy, connected to others, and like you matter, you are on the right track. Conversely, if you feel alone, frenetic, anxious, ill, or depressed, chances are you are not doing what you are supposed to be doing. Something in your personal or professional life is out of balance.

In my life, the things that have brought the most happiness and abundance have not come from me being smarter, working harder, or toiling more. They have come from a place of surrender, a place of calm, of listening, of taking risks, and embracing the unknown. When I operate from a place of force and control, I may break even, but the reward is never worth the energy exerted. Like when I decided to leave the law firm, more joy and pleasant surprises have come when I've said, "Screw it! This feels right! I know I am going to freak out my dad or make people who know me think I am out of my mind, but I'm doing it anyway."

The book *The Blue Sweater* tells the story of Jacqueline Novogratz, founder and CEO of the Acumen Fund. It illustrates how following the flow of the universe and allowing it to carry us will guide us to where we are called to be in the world. Jacqueline grew up in Alexandria, Virginia. When she was a young girl, her uncle gave her a blue wool sweater that had zebras and Kilimanjaro across the chest.

It became her favorite piece of clothing because it symbolized Africa as a big and far-off place in contrast to her small world. Despite shopping for new school clothes each year, she wore it as often as possible until, in the late seventies, she finally grew out of it and donated it to Goodwill.

After high school, she attended the University of Virginia and had aspirations to be of service to the poor, to support those less fortunate all over the world. Sometime after graduation, she moved to Latin America for a position in commercial banking.

After a few years of working in this capacity, she took a consulting job with UNICEF in Kigali, Rwanda.[2] While there, she helped establish a microfinance enterprise for poverty-stricken women. In order to embark on this journey, she had to leave behind the comforts of living in America; she had to step outside her comfort zone and surrender to the unknown.

While jogging one day through the streets of Rwanda, Jacqueline saw a young boy approaching her. He was wearing a familiar-looking sweater. She could see it was made of blue wool with zebras at the foot of Kilimanjaro. Excitedly, she ran up to the boy and turned down his collar to see her name written on the tag. It was the sweater she'd donated over a decade earlier. The blue sweater had somehow made its way to him, all the way in Africa.[3] In that moment, she felt a deep sense of universal connectivity. By letting go and using *wu wei*, she was led to Africa, where she would become a vessel for impacting significant change.

I believe adherence to *wu wei* is essential to reaching our full potential. I often evaluate whether or not I am going out for the run, tying up my shoes, and allowing the wind to guide my course. If I am pushing a head wind, I know I am operating outside of *wu wei*. If that is the case, I turn around and head in the direction of ease. This might mean I stop trying to force a business deal or that I have flexibility in how my children and I spend our weekend. It might mean I don't get worked up over a missed flight and instead just book another. In society, however, these kinds of *go with the flow* techniques are antithetical to running a business. Many of us believe that if things are not flowing and the best course of action is to push the pause button on billing, then somehow, we are giving up by doing so. Similarly, deciding to put new people on a project or acknowledging to the client that we didn't have everything configured at the onset looks like weakness to the ego. The truth is making these adjustments and admitting to not being in flow is how we grow. It is what puts us on the right track.

The ego doesn't subscribe to the idea of flow. It is that very real part of us that strives to make its presence known. It says, "I have to do this. I have to control. I don't need help." It is that part of us which feeds off of praise, compliments, and success, and so wants to do all the work itself. It believes this is how it will get the glory.

I view the ego in the Jungian way, as being our multiple parts, our multiple personalities. These parts that run the show vary from person to person, depending on life experience. For instance, if you grew up in a home of alcoholism, chances are the parts of your ego will function out of a need to fend for yourself. They will emerge from a place of fear and control. This is not a bad thing but requires examination and awareness. It requires maturity to know when to call forth those personality traits and when to store them away. Each of our parts has a valuable role to play and is absolutely welcome and needed at the table. At the same time, we must remember they are not meant to run the show.

Take Blake Mycoskie, founder and CEO of TOMS shoes, for example. Although he is the CEO of the iconic brand, he is also the chairman of Blake Mycoskie, the person behind the business. He is the person in charge of his every action and his every pursuit. As a whole and centered being, he has the ability to invite any one of his ego parts to sit at the boardroom table. He should be able to honor the chief operating officer within—that part of him that worries about whether the electrical bill is going to get paid and if processes are in place so business and life flow optimally. Then there is the chief marketing officer part of him. He makes sure that he and his business are seen, that neither get lost in the crowd. He is the part of Blake that connects with others in social media and through brand messaging. He is the part that connects with the outside world to establish relationships. Blake should never want to cut him out, but he certainly shouldn't want him running the show. Also in Blake's psyche is a general counsel—the voice and personality within that reminds him of inherent risks that exist in our world. It alerts him to those things that could cause everything he's built to be taken away. It makes sure he has policies, procedures, and practices in place to insulate him and his company from risk.

The general counsel of Blake sometimes has good insights, but if it ran the show, he'd constantly be living in fear. All of these guys sit day after day in the psychological boardroom with him. Depending on where Blake is or what he is doing at any particular moment, one or more of these boardroom members gets airtime. They each have a role. Their roles are important, and again, consciously or subconsciously, Blake listens to all of them. It is by being the chairman of his own identity and tuning in to the guidance and perspective of his various parts that he can make the decisions that best support his brand and company.

Living *wu wei* provides infinite possibilities and the highest amount of co-creation, so long as you remain the chairman. I often see two ways in which people let their parts run the show. One way is when businesses, or people, allow themselves to be in complete surrender to their chief operating officer. These are the people who are chronically toiling to make all the elements align. They are frenetic about timely bill paying, access to food, and household care and upkeep. They are in constant worry, continually preparing for the machine to break down at any time. Then there are the people who let their chief marketing officer run the show. They are generally pompous and want to be in the limelight. They get high off of big press releases and engage in a multitude of superficial interactions. Emptiness inside drives them to be seen and heard. They act in order to fill a void. In contrast, those of us who are working toward running our businesses and our lives with advice from our various inputs live in alignment with *wu wei*. We get to co-create with the universe, rather than co-creating with the multiple parts of our ego.

Wu wei is mindfulness. It is asking, *Is this a part of me?* It's questioning, *Am I in flow or is my ego in control?* This mindfulness takes discipline, practice, and self-awareness. It's not easy to go with the flow—despite phrases like *just go with the flow* permeating our vernacular. It's challenging but authentic. Once you begin to play with this construct, it ceases to be hard in terms of your level of toil. You still have to make the effort to stay rooted, but the reward is worth it. Living with *wu wei* is being able to call forth what is needed at any moment and not carry the baggage from history with us. It's focusing our attention where it will have the most impact with the least amount of effort.

A word of caution—your ego is going to try to tell you that, in order to reap the benefits of *wu wei*, you have to do it perfectly. Listen to its perspective and then, from your centered self, understand this is not true. You can and should experiment with it. You don't need to become a *wu wei* master right out of the gate. Start small. Perhaps a friendship that is one-sided or draining you of energy needs to receive less attention. Perhaps a project you are having trouble getting off the ground needs to be reconfigured. Start small and play around with not needing a particular result. Look for synchronicities and signs and then heed them. In my experience, once you start down this path and see results, you start to have fun with it. Before you know it, flow happens naturally.

9

INVOKING ARCHETYPAL ENERGIES:
What We Can Learn From Myth

"Every myth is psychologically symbolic.
Its narratives and images are to be read, therefore,
not literally, but as metaphors."
—Joseph Campbell

You may have had mythology as part of your curriculum in either high school or college. Perhaps you read Homer's *Odyssey* or the *Iliad*. When I read these works, they fascinated me. The skilled weaving of many stories into one captured and held my interest. Yet even though mythology was one of my favorite courses in high school, I did not have an understanding of why these stories resonated with me so deeply.

It wasn't until my years in college that I came to understand why reading such wordy and lengthy tales gave me a high. It was more than just skilled writing and godly characters that drew me in. As I was exposed to the brilliant works of Joseph Campbell, it was revealed to me that myth is the collective unconscious reduced to story and the real-life application of these stories is what really turned me on. Campbell believed mythical characters act as archetypes to demonstrate human possibility. No matter the medium, in the stories we know so well, we see heroes embodying archetypal energies and overcoming life's challenges.

We can learn the story of Luke Skywalker, of Arjuna from the *Bhagavad Gita*, or even of Merlin, and when confronted with challenges, we'll see ways we can also navigate our own lives. It is good to identify with these heroes, because there is so much to learn from them, and these myths not only instruct us, but they also show us we are not alone in our journeys. We are guided by them and comforted by them. They are somehow universal and unique at the same time.

Myth tells the tales of familiar themes woven into the fabric of our individual and collective lives. It brings to light the constructs that are inherent to us despite cultural differences, religion, geography, and spiritual practices. Myth tells the stories of good and evil, of God and creation. It provides context to the burdens and demands placed on our human existence. It answers the big questions like why we are here and why certain hardships occur in our lives. It makes sense of the ambiguity of our existence.

Traditionally, the natural human process for answering these questions has been to pontificate or debate with a friend or colleague. Historically, we humans have scrutinized with therapists or congregated in churches to read scriptures for our enlightenment. What we have not recognized, however, is that in order to answer life's most poignant questions, all we have to do is turn to myth. The main characters of our collective unconscious that are illustrated in story are archetypes. They are there for us to identify with and to learn from. Recognizing this, mythology can be very useful in our personal lives and in our business endeavors.

Mythology permeates and unites every culture, religion, and geography, and so we are all intimately familiar with its archetypes whether we know it or not. An archetype is an example, sometimes even the perfect example, of a particular type of something, in this case, people. When we look at the stories that have permeated our culture, we see archetypes everywhere, showing us by their actions what we can also aspire to.

In Judeo-Christianity, archetypes are saints. You may be familiar with Saint Michael the Archangel, the patron saint of the sick, or Saint Thomas the Apostle, the saint of overcoming doubt. Just like in Greek and Roman mythos, there are applicable stories about these Christian saints found in scripture. If you want to be of more service in your life, you can learn how by reading about Christ or Mother Teresa, and then invoke behaviors in sync with their acts and selfless existence. Or maybe you want to summon qualities of a humble hero. You could then turn to the story of Moses, who was shrouded as a child from those who wished to take his life. He went on to face many trials in Egypt, atoned for the sins of the Egyptian people, and called upon the strength of God to carry him. He was courageous, valiant, and conquered tribulation amidst incredible strife, all while remaining humble.

Archetypes in Our Current World

I generally speak of Greek archetypes because I studied them most, but these archetypes are seen in stories and traditions of every culture from the Inuits to the Egyptians. In the Egyptian mythos, they worshiped Ra, the god of the sun, while the sun god worshipped by the Greeks was Helios. The Greek god of the forge was Hephaestus, and to the Romans, it was Vulcan. These archetypes draw so much from each other that comparisons are natural.

Native American cultures worship animals and elements of nature to invoke the essence of specific strengths and power into their lives. Frequently the origin of their names is found in nature. For example, the name Nita in Choctaw means "bear," and Wayra in Quechua is "the wind." In these cultures, to embody certain characteristics, they focus attention on an animal or a force of nature that resembles the desired quality. If one wishes to be a bit wilier, they might focus on the coyote; if they want to be blessed with speed, they may observe the cheetah and ask the spirit of that animal to manifest through them.

Mythology is a brilliant gift to us. It is a tool for answering troublesome life questions and for examining our various attributes. It allows us to observe the characteristics of those we admire and makes us aware of those parts of us we may wish to renounce. We see our own species acting out the behaviors of influential, and sometimes destructive, archetypes every day. For instance, we all know of a modern-day Prometheus, the character who stole fire from the gods and brought it to man. The modern Prometheus is the man or woman whose passion in life is to take from those who have and give to those who have not. It is the men and women of society who empower the meek.

Arachne is also a highly visible archetype today. In Greek mythology, Arachne was a weaver of beautiful fabrics. She was proud of her skills and could not stop boasting of her talent. She even declared herself more skilled a weaver than the goddess Athena. When Athena caught wind of Arachne's arrogant claims, she disguised herself as an old woman and paid Arachne a visit. The old woman advised Arachne not to be boastful and not to pretend that she was like one of the gods. Arachne was defiant and arrogant. She told the old woman she would challenge her to a weaving contest. Suddenly, the old woman transformed herself back into the radiant goddess Athena. Everyone kneeled to pay his or her respects, except for Arachne; she couldn't wait for the competition to begin. She was full of pride and vanity, and began weaving pictures that showed her disdain for the gods. This angered the goddess so much that she turned Arachne into a spider, so she could go on spinning forever.

Arachne embodied pride and set her intentions on vainglory. She is visibly among us in the form of those who care only for themselves; she is personified in those who are not concerned for the well-being of others. The qualities of Arachne are also present in those who spend an exorbitant amount of time and money on their appearance with very little, if any, concern for their inner well-being.

We also are very familiar with Icarus, the son of the master crafts-man Daedalus. Icarus attempted to escape from Crete with wings his father had made of wax and feathers. Daedalus instructed young Ica-rus to avoid flying too close to the sun, as the intense heat would melt his wings. Defiant, young Icarus boldly ignored his father. He attempted the impossible, and his wings melted, and he fell, drown-ing in the sea below. You can easily see this story becomes very real through anyone who acts as though they are invincible, those who are defiant and won't listen to authority, their peers, or most of all, their inner voice. They are the athletes, celebrities, neighbors, and associates who seek glory and as a result, dishonor their sport, their families, and their lives.

There have been many times throughout life that I have chan-neled Icarus and Arachne. I remember once saying to my therapist, "Rick, I have to remind myself that all I am is a flute through which God's breath blows."

He replied, "You know, David, that may be true, but there have been times in our work together that I have felt you believed you have a really amazing flute, that yours is better than anyone else's." He was right.

I am human, and there are times I fall prey to invoking the quali-ties of Icarus. There are times I have believed God chooses to only blow through my flute. Without knowing and understanding mytho-logical stories, I would lack the tools necessary to stir my awareness. I would not be able to see how I am sometimes the embodiment of Icarus. Observing these stories provides context for my life. Now, instead of attempting to fly to the sun with wings coated in wax, I can catch myself before I ascend and fall. With these tools, when I feel myself acting without grace, I can call on an archetype of humility. I can summon an archetype of honesty or call forth those who repre-sent reverence and gratitude.

Jung believed that the collective unconscious expresses itself in the form of these archetypes, and that they influence our feelings and actions. For years we have used symbols to tell stories, convey meanings, and help us explain why we're here, but now, we rely on psychology to do this; however, psychology doesn't take into account or fully understand the *psyche* or the *self*.

Knowing Your Archetypes

Jung felt our goal should be to achieve self-integration, a joining of our conscious and unconscious minds, so our unique potential and individual divinity might be uncovered. He approached much of his work with clients by examining their archetypes and asking who was present at different moments. Perhaps the client was invoking the archetype of Chiron. Chiron was wise and the only immortal centaur (half man and half horse) in Greek mythology. He had a sound set of values, which he shared by mentoring many of the Greek heroes.[1] Perhaps the client was invoking characteristics of prideful Arachne. Maybe they were more like Aphrodite, the archetype of love. If they were invoking Medusa, Jung may have asked them what it is in their life that they couldn't stop from looking at yet were fully aware was not good for them. It is wise to know who and what your Medusa is and then have the discipline to look away. Perseus had this foresight and discipline. He avoided looking at Medusa when he fought her and used his shield's reflection to fight and ultimately prevail over her. Like Perseus, if you are seeing areas in your life that are bringing irrefutable harm, you may want to ask to know your Medusa.

Examine who you are in your relationships. What archetype are you calling forth at any given time? Discover the archetype of your business partner or spouse to learn about their reality. If you are married to Athena yet are trying to approach her like she's Aphrodite, you may be struggling. Learn about what characteristics she embodies and what makes her tick. Then you can avoid trying to woo her with lace panties from Victoria's Secret when what she really wants is a cotton T-shirt and pair of boy shorts.

You have the tools to do this self-examination. They are all right there in story. This process and study of invoking archetypal behavior proved valuable in Jung's patients, and it will for you too. Deepak Chopra talks at length about our inherent ability to call forth an archetype and ask it to manifest through us. He says if there is an area of your life you want to put an intention around, do it with the engagement of archetypes.[2] If you want more love in your life, more wanderlust, or to be a kinder and more selfless contributor to society, then go find the archetypes that exude those characteristics. Meditate on the stories and context, and ask the archetypes to manifest through you. Believe me, it works, and there is an archetype for nearly all material constructs that you might have in your life.

Archetypes in Business

What most people haven't recognized is that archetypes permeate business. Take Intel for example. Intel stock trades at a very low multiple. It doesn't have a very high valuation relative to others in its peer group. I would say the archetype of Intel is one of security, risk mitigation, and holding on to what you have instead of innovating. Intel is quite akin to the archetype Sophrosyne, who was the goddess of moderation, self-control, temperance, restraint, and discretion.

Google, on the other hand, can be characterized as the archetype of innovation, of wizardry. They created something where nothing before existed. They can be likened to the archetype of Merlin, the man who was best known for being a master magician.

Apple is one of the most valuable companies in the world according to its market cap. They embody a mélange of technology, art, and vision. Their brand is akin to three distinct archetypes. First is Merlin, the wizard. He makes things happen that wouldn't otherwise occur under familiar laws of nature. The next is Apollo, the businessman who has powerful influence and the eyes of an eagle and whose every movement is precise. And the third is Poseidon, the artist, the visionary who, in an empty wasteland, created a whole world for himself. When someone buys an Apple product, doing so speaks volumes about the role they play in life. An Apple consumer buys for both design and functionality. They are drawn to the beauty and simplicity of the machine. When using an iPad during a business luncheon, they are making a statement.

PC consumers play a different role—not better or worse, just different. They just want to get their work done accurately and on time, and computers are tools to be used to accomplish a specific purpose. For them, there is little need for fluff or aesthetics. Function is the main focus. They are the Hercules of personal computers, the archetype of determination and strength.

Just like the relationship between consumer products and their archetypes, we can also be likened to archetypal energies. One, two, or three may be more prominent, but we can invoke as many as we choose in order to support us in any situation. I have discovered that I have a reasonable dose of Athena qualities. She is a planner, mediator, strategist, and rational thinker. She is fierce and brave in battle, but only when battle is necessary. And she reminds us to use our intellect as well as our creativity in the pursuit of any goal. She represents controlled strength, integration, and the power of *and*.

Another archetype I deeply resonate with is Hermes. He is the good shepherd and mediator of information as it crosses from the subconscious to the conscious mind. He confidently conveys the messages that pass between these two realms. Writing this book has been an inspired work, one I know I have been called to complete and share with you. As much as I have, at times, felt insecure about delivering the content of these pages, as well as fearful it wouldn't be received by open minds, I have surrendered to the call to write. I've known I have an important message to share, and in order to feel more confident in doing so, I have invoked Hermes's communication qualities.

Professionally, you might say I could be likened to Merlin. Merlin is the wizard that uses knowledge of the world and real-life experience to solve problems. In my business relationships, I draw on my own experience as well as those of my partners to help clients overcome inherent entrepreneurial challenges. Through invoking Merlin, I can inspire them to enter the unknown with confidence and combat trials with grace, and I can support them in becoming heroes of their own lives.

In order for us each to answer our unique heroic callings, we need to be open to and call upon our archetypal characteristics to guide us through the unknown. We need to learn to invoke the qualities that will best shape our behaviors and interactions. When we do, we are better able to move forward with clarity. If you are more inclined to function using logic, process, and intellect but could benefit from more creative characteristics, perhaps invoke the qualities of Metis, the Greek goddess who is wise, artistic, and the one-time lover of Zeus. She uses creativity to craft objects from intuition. You could also invoke the empathetic characteristics of Demeter, the Greek goddess of the harvest who took great interest in the well-being of those around her.

It is through studying archetypes that we can come to know their various qualities, strengths, and weaknesses. We can learn to invoke the characters' energies and as a result, gain a deeper understanding of how to blend leadership, innovation, and creativity—or applicability, dedication, and methodology. We can learn how and when to simply listen and when it's better to engage. We can learn how to invoke empathy and compassion and when logic and analytics are useful in formulating a plan. It is by implementing this tool that we become more relatable and more in control of our behaviors.

Calling on archetypes can help us when engaging others in a professional capacity. It is useful to recognize that those who are involved in enterprise contribute significantly to the brand and its products and services. To understand one's vision and values, we can examine:

- the archetypal energies that most clearly define the company and what they offer, and
- what the most prominent archetypal energies of the founder, staff, and consultants are. (They are often not the same. Depending on who you are engaging at any one company, they may affirm the main priority of their brand is innovation, yet personally, they may be focused on goodwill.)

Knowing this, we can find common ground with the people we engage with. When addressing a client, vendor, or potential partner, you might ask questions such as: If you are interested in innovation and creativity, would you say you are somewhat of a wizard? This kind of questioning gets them thinking about a character type you both can understand and speak about. This is a great exercise for getting clear about the characteristics and qualities of a brand, product, or services. It helps you gain a mutual understanding of the qualities that can help mold and shape the relationship going forward.

When I ask founders what their vision, their personal primary objective, is, I may get a very different answer from what their intention is for their business. Perhaps it is to amass wealth. If it is, there are archetypes that represent wealth that are instructive. It may be wise for the founder to study an archetype of acquiring wealth, a King Midas for example. In doing so, they may come to learn how such a priority could lead them down an undesirable path if their intentions were not grounded in well-being. Or maybe their mission in life is to be of service to others. This is a beautiful quality that could be supported by invoking the strategic and intellectual energy of Athena.

The best businesses understand how to integrate these archetypes. Again, Dave of Dave's Killer Bread invoked the archetype of redemption, of the redeemed. His story and brand is one of redemption and forgiveness. It is the story of the Phoenix, which every five hundred years, consumes itself in fire and is born again. Dave's story is not just about freedom from prison, but also prison in the mythological sense, and the notion that we all, at times, are confined to our own penitentiaries. As a result, the myth is able to penetrate the consumer. It says that no matter who you are and no matter what prison you are in, you can break free. You can be Dave. You can manifest freedom in your life. These are powerful stories. They are valuable tools meant for integration into our lives. Brands that get this and play to it by building a brand message and a promise rooted in mythos have greater success at capturing and nurturing their consumer, thereby creating lasting brand loyalty.

Another archetype we often see in business is that of the philanthropist. Using TOMS Shoes as an example again, Blake's brand promise is *One for One*. For every pair of shoes you purchase, TOMS gives a pair of new shoes to a child in need. This resonates at a cellular depth because we, at some collective-conscious level, like equality. We deeply value the comfort of all beings. TOMS brand message speaks to that. They do so knowingly, and it captures the consumer. When people buy Nike, they are invoking qualities of Zeus. When consumers buy Victoria's Secret, it's because they resonate with and desire to invoke the qualities of Aphrodite. What is fascinating is this is all happening on a subconscious level. Generally, neither the company nor the consumers are aware it is happening; they are both often unaware of why such a solid relationship has been built.

One of my favorite examples of mythos and archetypal energy at work in business is yogitoes. Founder Susan Nichols, who I spoke of before, is undeniably the embodiment of beauty, goddess energy, and femininity. These qualities are matched by yang, a masculine energy. She has straightforwardness and power that allows her to own and operate a very successful business. Susan could be likened to an Amazonian goddess, a beautiful woman who frolics around waterfalls and runs by the side of a tranquil river. The same woman who has a bow and arrow quiver behind her back. She can shoot that arrow straight as a laser and zap you right between the eyes.

Her brand and product line, yogitoes, could be likened to the archetype of the warrior princess. A combination of Athena and Aphrodite, the warrior princess is capable of winning a fight, but she is also stunningly beautiful, amazingly feminine, and incredibly soft. Yogitoes embodies that incredible combination. Their yoga towels are the warrior princess. They come in an array of beautiful colors and feminine designs but are made for the type of yoga that causes you to sweat two liters in a single class. You take one look at the towel and think, *Oh, such a dainty and pretty little towel,* then all of a sudden, the yogi whips it out, spreads it on their mat, and goes to town in a ninety-minute hot vinyasa class. The towel becomes a tool of strength. It allows the yogi to dig into their asana practice and power through a class, even when they are dripping sweat from every pore.

Studying myth and learning to invoke archetypes can be a powerful tool for helping us find common ground with others and for evolving our personal and professional activities. By weaving archetypal energy into our language, corporate cultures, and life, we are better able to navigate interactions and challenges. By examining archetypal energies, by reading mythological stories, we gain the ability to follow a trail of thinking much further. As we travel down that path, we find we each have these tools within us, which further shapes our brands and nurtures our relationships.

Whether in your personal journey, with family or business, look at the archetypes you want to manifest. Understand them and read the myths that contain those archetypes. Then meditate on them. Ask the universe to invoke them and make them present in your life. Do so purposefully. Play with blending the qualities of multiple archetypes. Some days, you may invoke two ounces of Merlin, three of

Zeus, and one of Dionysus. Another day, maybe you'll want to invoke the creative qualities of Metis. Be aware of the characters you are invoking subconsciously and learn to manage resulting behaviors. In doing so, your business will thrive. Your relationships will thrive. You will thrive.

10

CONSCIOUS COMMUNICATION:
The Convergence of Myth, Psychology, Science, Religion, and Our Universal Language

"It is not a good idea to be well adjusted to a
profoundly sick society."

—Jiddu Krishnamurti

Since the beginning of time, the ideas and concepts I have shared throughout this book have permeated all aspects of spirituality as well as our everyday lives. Embracing oneness, living in flow, trusting and surrendering, embracing our shadow, living our dharma, heeding our call, co-creating, integrating, and manifesting are ancient precepts brought forth by virtually every wisdom and tradition. We, as Westerners, have deemed many of these principles "woo-woo" and have confined them to religion and spirituality. But as you have seen in these chapters, the same ideals for living are present across all ideologies. All of the constructs within these pages can be seen in quantum physics, art, philosophy, and spirituality; they are just described in different ways. For example, in spirituality, we talk about manifestation while in religion the same theme is called miracles. In philosophy or myth, the construct is referred to as the gods at work and in psychology, the workings of the mind. The universal theme of oneness is exhibited in each of these disciplines differently, yet they are all speaking the same language.

Our Labels

Our human mind likes to break things down, to contextualize and put ideas, people, and things into tidy boxes. Doing so helps us better understand what can initially be mentally overwhelming. It also allows us to establish boundaries, to draw big, fat lines of safety around who we are, and to help make sense of our existence. This human approach to making sense of things limits our ability to expand. It limits our ability to evolve as a species. You have been exposed to these universal themes in mythological stories. For eons, philosophers, mythologists, scientists, psychologists, priests, and artists have all been sharing these same universal truths. They have been spreading the same message, just using a different language to do so.

Physicists have spoken of matter, particles, and the elements to describe what the mystics call co-creation. If you study the Heisenberg uncertainty principle, you will discover its core fundamentals are those of manifestation. The same is true of the observer effect. You see these constructs are not new age; they are not "woo-woo." They have been with us since we crawled from the primordial soup. It is the ego that likes to label and define.

These mythological stories and those I have shared throughout these pages have helped me realize how important it is for us to unite in our connectedness, including our language and theories of creation. I have realized that to truly live our most authentic and abundant lives, we have to learn a universal language. We have to embrace the lexicon of truth. This is no small task and is going to take a bit of reprogramming, as the only language we have known is one of separation. Let it be understood that this is no fault of our own. Until now, we weren't fully awake. As Alan Watts said, "We seldom realize that our most private thoughts and emotions are not actually our own. For we think in terms of languages and images which we did not invent, but which were given to us by our society."[1]

We are awake now, however, which means we have a choice in where we go from here. We have a choice to celebrate our unity, wholeness, and essential heritage. We can and should choose to emerge from the confines of our cultural containers. These containers run the gamut from our fields of work, level of wealth, relationship status, age, and even the neighborhoods we live in. We have gone so far as to categorize ourselves by diet types. We are known to say, "I am a vegetarian" or "He is paleo." If you really stop and think about it, what we are literally saying is "I am a diet."

It has been so easy for us to surrender to the ignorance of the ego and label all things around us, including our beliefs. But now that we are expanding as a species, we are beginning to speak openly and accurately of our oneness. We are embracing the themes of living I have shared, which support a new way of existing, of being in service to ourselves and all beings everywhere. Eckhart Tolle in *A New Earth* said, "When you don't cover up the world with words and labels, a sense of the miraculous returns to your life that was lost a long time ago when humanity, instead of using thought, became possessed by thought."[2]

Accepting Our *And*

Collectively, we have entered a new state of consciousness and more of us are embracing the timeless truths I have shared in this book. We are seeing examples of this new state of mind in advertising and across the web, such as Ford's ad for their 2014 Fusion Hybrid that boldly speaks to the power of *and*. It opens with a driver and passenger discussing how the Fusion gets great gas mileage *and* looks good, which they say is much better than having to choose between good looks *or* great gas mileage. The passenger then suggests that having to choose between aesthetics and miles per gallon is just as ridiculous as someone being large *or* in charge. The ad then transitions into a scene where a shrunken down, three-inch man standing on top of a conference table is pointing his finger and shouting at a group of normal-sized colleagues. The ad is making the point that being large *or* in charge is ineffective, emphasizing the fact that *and* is better.[3]

Not only are we seeing the power of *and* permeating mainstream media, but also inspirational quotes from everyone including the Dalai Lama to Albert Einstein are peppering users' Facebook and Twitter profiles. This is happening as our collective consciousness demands the authentic expression of our beliefs in compassion, mindfulness, and unity. We're even seeing content writers and contributors to the *Wall Street Journal, New York Times,* and *Huffington Post* delivering content that speaks to meditation, collective consciousness, living in the present, and manifestation.

On the *Mind Openerz* website, an article shares how scientists have proven DNA can be reprogrammed by words and frequencies,[4] and on September 7, 2013, the *New York Times* published an article about how there are gifts and lessons to be learned from suffering.[5] This mass awareness and people's desire to share their beliefs are spreading at a rate faster than ever before. Messages of oneness, compassion, and well-being are replacing those of separatism and self-gratification. Collectively, we are accepting the truth that at the core of our very beings are simple and applicable tools to help us on our journey. You, by the mere fact of choosing to read this book, have tapped into this awareness. Maybe you arrived here from a feeling that our society was digressing, that with the economic collapse, broken families, rising obesity, and divorce rates, we were headed straight into self- and collective destruction.

The truth is, we were, but due to more of us waking up to these simple truths, we have turned a corner and possibly, without knowing, have begun a wave of dramatic human evolution. In doing so, we have said yes to exploring a new way of thinking. We have chosen to consider there is a better way to operate in all areas of our existence, even advancing this awareness in our careers and business life. Something is moving us to seek greater knowledge. Knowledge of what is really true for us, and all the while we are developing a language that best expresses our emerging deep wisdom.

Little by little, our once-casual conversations are evolving into heart-centered and awe-inspiring discussions about this simple fact. As we evolve, we are beginning to feel free to express our desires for more harmony, fun, abundance, love, and joy—in both our work and relationships. What is brilliant is that not only do we desire these inborn gifts, but we also believe wholeheartedly that we can have them all. We trust they are ripe and ready for harvesting. It is this belief that is responsible for birthing our new state of being.

As we live with greater awareness and observation, our collective vibration is providing direct access to pure potential. By focusing our attention on this whole new state of being, we are beginning to intuit a higher meaning. We are inherently gaining a heightened sense of our role in the world and becoming more mindful of our thoughts, actions, and speech. As we become more present to the vibrations of our interactions, we are evaluating how we are relating to others and ourselves. We are stopping to ask if we are expanding or contracting and wondering if our actions are increasing or decreasing our life force. We are beginning to question how we are speaking and if the language we are using is appropriate for our new level of cosmic understanding.

As we reawaken, we are beginning to realize that spiritual laws are actually universal truths that apply to every aspect of life. And we're beginning to realize that we are ready for monumental change in our lives. In the past decade, there has been a convergence of atrocities that have beaten us down so much that the only way out has been up. We have been witness to and victims of unemployment, seen millions of loved ones and colleagues die every year from preventable diseases like obesity and diabetes, and we've been burdened by corruption in government, rising tax rates, war, and famine. The universal truths I've been sharing are beating us over the head right now because we have hit rock bottom, and it's time for us to rise like the phoenix. Enough of us are tired of the way we have collectively been living, and if enough of us believe, we can and will shift consciousness and repair the world.

The Power of Language

The words we use can instruct, enlighten, inform, and comfort. They can also destroy, belittle, berate, and harm. There is power in our words and in the reasons we choose to use them. A few years back, I traveled to Montana for a weeklong trip into the Bob Marshall Wilderness Area. During my journey, I chose to take a scenic route and stopped for a bit at the shores of a lake. The thousands of trees that had obviously been cut down disheartened me. Just to the left of where I stood, there was a big sign posted by the forestry service. It read, "This timber has been harvested for your viewing pleasure." The sign did nothing to lessen my sadness over the destruction. I thought about the choice of phrasing, and it occurred to me that if they had selected words such as, "These trees have been cut down so you can see the lake better," it would have had a completely different effect on me as the reader. They intentionally chose less abrasive words to avoid upsetting people.

We see the conscious and unconscious selection of words all the time in our lives. For instance, there are those who cling to the words of their priest. They are so deeply moved when he talks about how, if we trust in God, miracles will abound in our lives. There are those who cleave to the words of their chosen spiritual leader while shunning parallel ideals presented by a leader whose word choice is unfamiliar.

Consider the Palestinian and the Jew. Imagine you put them on opposite sides of an arbitrary boundary with the Palestinian dressed in one color scarf and the Jew in another. By the slightest difference in appearance, they will shoot to kill each other. Yet, if you strip them of their clothes and put them in a room together, you may not be able to say what the differences between them are. It is abominable there is genocide over such menial differences. It is ludicrous that, like the artist who thinks the scientist is talking gibberish, we have historically chosen to focus on differentiating words. For far too long, we have lowered our states of being to that of words, and in doing so, we have failed to accept our universal language. This has caused considerable disconnection and suffering among humanity. It has resulted in the mass destruction of our world and lives. If we all approached our lives from a place of integration and understood that what we each speak about is coming from a single source, these constructs for living would go a long way toward repairing the world.

Unfortunately, we have only known how to function with a local language that we have learned. Yet, as we evolve, we learn to speak with integrity and only of that which is universally true and accurate, but only when what we have to say is more beautiful than silence do we evolve. Our speech and selection of words must become a practice in mindfulness, and as a result, we'll know no judgment or separation.

Language is originally and essentially just a system of signs and symbols which denote real occurrences or echo in the human soul. The universal languages of music, touch, body language, a smile, and those of our common, shared existence have always existed, but somewhere along our journey, they were fragmented by the ignorance of our ego.

A New Vocabulary

Scientologists have developed and speak their own language. It is so specialized that they had to print a dictionary to translate all of their words. L. Ron Hubbard, the man who founded Scientology, made this a priority so followers would use precise terminology and avoid confusion with words that have other meanings. Their terminology is so unique and precise, it has been likened to math.

I am not suggesting we rewrite the dictionary, nor am I praising Scientology; rather, I am emphasizing the importance of having a precise language that supports our evolution—and I am emphasizing that we must all learn this language to better support our unity. To articulate further, let me share a couple of examples of old, unconscious, and inaccurate phrases. Both are common to our Western language yet are no longer aligned with our heightened level of consciousness. Take the overused phrase *mind-body connection*. The use of the word connection implies separation. In our new way of thinking and speaking, we understand that, since there is no separation between body and mind, there cannot be a connection. Rather, the accurate phrase is *mind-body oneness*. Similarly, the use of the word *leadership* is also one of an old paradigm. It connotes that there are sheep and there are herders. Again, it implies separation. It suggests there is an elite figure that presides over someone that is less than. Leadership can and should be replaced with heroism, because we are all equally the heroes of our own lives.

Do you see how such a subtle shift in the way we speak helps ensure accurate articulation of our existence? Being mindful of phrasing and the communication of ideas is essential to the evolution of the human condition. As we become keen observers of our thoughts, actions, and words, we begin to eradicate ignorance and miscommunication.

We need to begin speaking the language of intuition, the language of rightness and truth, extinguishing those ideas and words that separate us. We can be mindful of our words and repel those that creep in unconsciously or as a result of habit. It would behoove us to speak words of purity, as doing so requires pure thought. Words like *sustainability* need to be left behind. *Advertising Age* named sustainability one of the "jargoniest jargon" words of 2010, calling it "a good concept gone bad by mis- and overuse." The list was subtitled "Here's a List of Words We Wish You'd Stop Saying," and I agree.[6] Besides, who wants to only live a sustainable life or have a sustainable relationship with their child? By its very nature, this word limits possibility. It is more consciously evolved to say one wants *life-affirming* relationships and experiences. In the world of commerce, a corporation would apply this understanding by saying, "Our business practices are life-affirming."

Additionally, the use of the term *power of and* is paramount for us to continue advancing as a species. Speaking about the integration of ideas and principles is universally correct. Doing so helps unite us, ending the suffering we have inflicted upon ourselves from a mindset of duality and the tyranny of *or*. We must also welcome *whole-brain consulting* and *intuitive analytics* into the language of commerce. These constructs and phrases replace old and stodgy "right-brain" versus "left-brain" phrasing as they relate to business.

At Meriwether, we use phrases like the *art of the agreement*. The underpinnings of this phrase contextualize how integrating finesse and grace contributes to mutual satisfaction. Similarly, intuitive analytics balance empathy, patience, finesse, compassion, and creativity with logic, analytics, and process. It results in more than just a transaction; it ensures transformation and a positive outcome for all parties. And, by doing business with mutual benefit in mind, we practice *compassionate commerce*.

This more evolved way of speaking has been used throughout time, but has rarely been applied to consumerism or the world of business. The reemergence of this accurate language is shaping and redefining what has traditionally been relegated to spirituality, art, science, philosophy, and mythology. We have now put it into a more relevant lexicon to be applied to commerce in the same way we apply it to our personal interactions. As more heroes in industry opt to choose their language wisely, we will expand our possibilities. As corporations and small businesses alter the way they brand to be more universally aligned, they will create a change in commerce, which will result in a powerful ripple effect, commanding greater change in the world. A more vibrationally comfortable interaction will be created between the consumer and the products and services they elect to buy. At a core level, this will fundamentally change the world.

All of these universal laws and ideas are being supported by modern-day science. Physicists and scientists are discovering what sages, yogis, shamans, rabbis, priests, and philosophers have always known. They are proclaiming with certainty that we are all interconnected, that we are truly entangled in a single universal web (called *quantum entanglement*, as discussed before). In *The Tao of Physics*, Fritjof Capra tells us that quantum theory is a scientifically sound and elegant expression of the relationship between the observer and the observed universe, which, as implied by the word *uni*verse, is, in truth, one unified field of pure consciousness.[7]

When we come to understand the interplay of all things, we immediately know how our actions, big or small, affect the cosmos. Who we are at any given moment and how we treat others and ourselves directly impacts the well-being of all creatures everywhere. Our existence is multidimensional. We live in an infinite reality and one with infinite possibilities, no matter how deep of a mindless hole we may have dug ourselves into. Together, since our vibrations of energy are so strong and our bonds unbreakable, we can now realize how we effect greater change. We do this by observing and becoming ever more mindful of our actions, words, and deeds. And we do this by accepting our oneness, speaking the pure universal language of awareness, and taking responsibility for our role in the collective imprint.

We cannot run from these truths and recent discoveries. If joy and abundance are desires we share, it is essential we rewire and reprogram our perceived separateness and transform it into oneness.

It is time to download a new vocabulary and way of processing ideas about who we are and why we are here. In order to evolve, we need to liberate ourselves from old paradigms and the confines of our learned thoughts and language. There are limitations to our rational thinking, and it is ultimately our intuitive wisdom that will set us free. As we act consciously, we will no longer need to look outside ourselves for value, happiness, and strength. We will no longer feel compelled to look to our partners to feel whole, to friends for a compliment, a job or diet to define our identity, or our experiences to mold and shape who we are. We will come to know we have everything we need within our very being and that, by being plugged into the collective unconscious, we are all heroes of our own life-affirming existence.

Part III

MASTERY

11

YOUR DEFINING MOMENT
AND THE RETURN:
The Hero Is You

"He who does not get fun and enjoyment out of every day . . .
needs to re-organize his life."

—George Matthew Adams

The dictionary has a number of definitions for *hero*, the first having to do with mythological and legendary archetypes, leaving us with visions of dragon slayings and saving the world from an ever-ensuing darkness. Yet one definition stands out to me: "an object of extreme admiration or devotion."[1]

Believing you are a hero may seem like something out of a fairy tale; if the idea does not seem impossible to intuit, you may feel that, by embracing this truth, you will be called to carry a heavy load of responsibility. For some of you, that may be true. Yet, regardless of how heavy a burden you may be called to bear or the grandiosity of the legacy you may leave behind, you are a hero on every level. As Joseph Campbell said in an interview with Bill Moyers, "A hero is someone who has given his or her life to something bigger than oneself."[2] You say yes to your heroism when you choose to live authentically, love yourself, accept your divinity, and share your light with the world.

The Sanskrit word *namaste*, which is spoken at the close of most yoga classes, is more than just a salutation. It literally means "I bow to you," and it is done as a gesture of acknowledgment to show that the divine soul in you bows to and honors the divine soul in others. This truth was echoed in Chardin's simple yet powerful statement quoted earlier: "We are spiritual beings having a human experience." We are all divine; we are all souls who have taken up residency in the shell of a body. This truth should be reason enough to embrace your heroism. Being a hero does not translate to your slaying evil or rescuing a princess from a dark fate. It does not mean you set out to defeat the Death Star or to destroy the evil witch. Those are stories meant to explain and contextualize the essence of being a hero, which is living authentically and staying true to who you are and to your soul's purpose. This may mean you are a farmer; it may mean you are a parent, a poet, a fisherman, an engineer of roads and highways, an athlete, or a politician. It may mean you clean homes or are a nanny, a nurse, a teacher, or an executive.

Acceptance of your divinity and living your purpose takes constant practice. I have lost my way many times and burned my hero's cloak. Even while writing this book, I have been wrought with fear, self-doubt, and a tremendous amount of insecurity. As I composed each chapter, limiting thoughts like *Who am I to share this message?* and *Why would anyone want to hear or read anything I have to say?* have crept in many times. Such thoughts have permeated my internal dialogue.

Yet, despite the ego mind chatter, I forged on, knowing these thoughts are not real. It is the nature of our minds to limit our beliefs and renounce our divinity. The ego kicks in, as does traditional Western thought, and says a heroic purpose is too daunting, or it tells us that we are just average people, not heroes. Yet if we truly stop and listen, if we quiet our minds long enough, we will come to understand and learn there is cosmic power in each of us. As Lao Tzu said,

"Without going outside, you may know the whole world. Without looking through the window, you may see the ways of heaven. The farther you go, the less you know. Thus the sage knows without traveling; he sees without looking; he works without doing."[3] The divine is not external and separate from us. It is within and all around us. We need to trust it and let it flow; we need to be the flute through which God's breath blows.

Our Unique Hero Roles

How we play out the role of hero will vary. Our personal journeys are unique. We have each been given individual skills, gifts, and abilities that shape our various contributions to the world. No calling is too great or too small. Each and every summons is special and powerful in its own way, and it may not be until the end of our lives that our purpose is made known. In some cases, we may never know. My wife, Heather, has had an adventurous spirit all her life. This zeal prompted her to study the most difficult language she could in high school: Chinese. Her teacher, a slight and scholarly man, was a patient and skilled teacher, and as a result of his teaching, Heather excelled in her studies. Upon graduation, she took a job in Hong Kong to teach English at a university. At about the same time, her teacher returned to China and taught there. Heather went to go see him one afternoon, and he shared some very unfortunate news with her.

Upon his return from the United States, authorities approached him, saying his teaching was too westernized, and as a result, they were sending him to an "education camp." Heather could see the fear in his eyes and, without a second thought, took him by the hand. They exited the university and made their way to the consulate, where she married him. She did this knowing he would be allowed to live safely in America. For her, this meant she would be legally bound to him for the next two years. The length of their union was of no concern to her.

All she knew was she was heeding a prompt to help. She purchased an airline ticket on her parent's American Express, and he was on a flight to the United States the next morning. Following the dissolution of their legal binding, they vowed to move on in their separate lives. Years later, Heather does not know what became of him, but she can hope the heroic actions she took that day saved his life.

We never know what we will be called to do, but we must engage and heed our call no matter what. Our journey may appear to be unimportant; it could also appear to be profound. In both cases, the result is equally meaningful. Throughout Heather's life, she may have not thought much of her choice to marry her teacher. To her, it may have seemed insignificant, yet he may say she was a literal lifesaver.

Frodo Baggins, the primary hero in *The Lord of the Rings* trilogy, could have also been viewed as an unlikely hero before readers understood his calling. He was an ordinary hobbit whose life was simple and quiet. To many, he may have even seemed insignificant, but when called upon to be a hero, his light side, his divinity was so strong that he was the perfect choice for that role. His mission to take the ring to Mordor so it could finally be destroyed was incredibly dangerous, but it also involved much more than what he encountered along the way. The real danger was in carrying the ring—known to corrupt anyone who came in contact with it—without giving in to its temptations. Frodo was fully aware he was sacrificing himself in hopes the world would be saved. Not unlike any hero's call, as he made his way, he was met with a crew of mentors. As he journeyed, he encountered his mentors and guides. Eight companions in total showed up to support him in his journey to destroy the ring and defeat Sauron, the Dark Lord.

Samwise Gamgee, known as Sam, was Frodo's gardener and filled the archetypal role of the sidekick. As Frodo became weak by the heavy burden of carrying the ring, Sam stepped up to help out. He carried luggage, cooked their meals, and often kept watch at night. He embodied the heroic qualities of courage and care. He and the others who supported Frodo called themselves the Fellowship of the Ring. Each of those accompanying Frodo on his journey imparted valuable gifts and supported each other during their journey through their many trials. In this tale, not only was Frodo heeding his call and fulfilling his journey, but those in the Fellowship were too; they were all called to be heroes.

Look at Vincent van Gogh. He also does not fit the typical hero profile. It was his honest commitment to expressing the spiritual essences of the natural world through his art and touching so many lives that qualifies him as a hero. Van Gogh lived a tragic life. He was socially awkward, suffered from mental illness, and died by his own hand. He was misunderstood by many, and even his own mother threw away several of his paintings. During his time on earth, he sold only one painting, reaching the status of art icon only after his death.

Today, of course, his work is recognized worldwide and sells for millions. Through his art, van Gogh revolutionized our perception of the world. Before modern physics was able to articulate that everything is energy in a web of interconnectedness, I believe van Gogh painted it for us.

Accepting Our Heroism

We are not here to question intuition, nor are we here to wrestle with our call. Sometimes we must think fast, and in other cases, we are not to think at all. In all cases, we are meant to go with the flow. We are meant to accept the truth that embarking on our journey, despite how grand or insignificant it may seem, is what life is all about.

By heeding our calling and staying true to our individual life paths, we create *tikkun olam*. We repair the world. We do this by returning to our divinity and knowing we are all doing God's work. Unfortunately, until now, we have been living our lives from a place of separateness and accepting ourselves as less than divine. There is still time, however, to shift our awareness. It is not too late to accept our divinity and repair the world. To do it, we need to stop looking outside ourselves for heroes. Rather than looking for them in churches and synagogues, corporations, government, or professional athletes, we need to look within. Rather than looking to societies and huge economic empires as leaders of heroism, all we need to do is look at ourselves.

My hope is that we will all come to live up to a mantra of truth like that of *namaste*. That it will sound something like, *I have the right and responsibility to consider my divine purpose and to be a light that will illuminate the world*, yoga instructor and friend, Josh Blatter once said, "From just one spark we can create one fire and from one fire we can create one light. From that one light, we create vision and that vision is how we share just one spark. Inspire all those around you."[4] This spark—our light, our vision—is what creates *tikkun olam*.

Real change in the world happens at the level of the individual. When enough of us start to believe we are heroes, when we reclaim our power and start living authentically, we inspire others to do the same. By our single spark, we create vision, and from that vision, we ignite one spark. When we all start living with purpose, meaning, honor, and gratitude, our light shines on our co-workers, our children, our friends, our neighbors, and even those we pass on the street. The ripple effect of conscious living begins to change the world. It is the only thing that *can* change the world. This is what the Old Testament meant when it talked about *ruach elohim*. It was telling us to recognize that the breath of God is the essential creative force and active power, and it is within each of us. In recognizing and tapping into that, we can change the world.

Fundamentally, if we all live a life of heroism, there can be no more famine. Environmental degradation will cease. Historically, we have limited ourselves and been held down. We have allowed ourselves to be sheep answering to the shepherd. We have allowed ourselves to be led. We need to move away from the leader-follower mentality and embrace heroism and authentic living.

If CEOs and management teams would begin to think of themselves more as heroes and less as chief executives, they would experience radical shifts in the culture of their businesses, meaningful shifts that would result in more joy, more ease in their day, and greater abundance. The Meriwether definition of an entrepreneur is anyone looking to catalyze change in the world by creating new and better ways for people to interact with their products, services, and each other. Entrepreneurs are the heroes of today—we are the heroes of our day. As executives and small business owners, we have an incredible opportunity to enhance the lives of thousands through our work. In doing so, our lives are also enriched. If we approach business more holistically and from a place of service, from a place of simply living our dharma and less from a place of ego and competition, we will create more fluidity in business.

There have been some business leaders who have exemplified this. Steve Jobs is one. He manifested beauty in the world by creating products that appeal to his consumer base on a deep and meaningful level. There are metrics in commerce showing that companies like Apple, who are true to their dharma and purpose, are shaping the future. There is a reason Apple is one of the most valuable companies in the world. It is because these ideals permeate the company's culture, their products, brand, and overall ethos. They remain true to the constructs that create value. In doing so, they and others like them attract the most consumers, define the biggest brands, and retain the best talent. In fulfilling their journey and being heroes of their lives and businesses, they bring the best out in their employees. They create cultures of innovation, of wanting to birth and push possibilities. Teams and employees thrive when they recognize each of them is divine. By the founder's example, employees come to know they are each tapped into the collective and what they have to offer, both individually and collectively, is needed, meaningful, and valuable.

It is these types of companies, these hero-minded founders that I choose to work with. Dave Dahl does business from the heart. He is filled with love and compassion and is on his journey, as are Susan of yogitoes and Lily of Pinto Barn. It is these companies that gain the respect of their consumers and peers and are making a difference in the world. They are living and operating their businesses authentically and by tapping into the collective unconscious, they know how to produce the goods and services humanity wants at exactly the time we begin to want them.

These are the individuals and companies who operate with integrity, and this level of honesty is desired by all of us, at our deepest core level. We want to know we can trust those selling to us, as well as those who advise us in how to run our businesses or who guide us in our consumerism. If you choose to integrate empathy, trust, surrender, the power of *and*, and the other tools I've shared in this book, you will be a hero of your business. You will be a hero of your own life.

By picking up and reading this book, you have taken steps toward embracing your heroism. I hope the messages I've shared will encourage you to integrate some of these tools and to put into action those you may already know so well, such as faith, the power of prayer, or yoga. I don't expect you to integrate them all, all at once. Maybe you simply begin by accepting you are divine and have a calling. Maybe you connect with the idea that, with trust and surrender, greater possibilities become inevitable. Maybe you will take with you the belief that we co-create our reality or that living from a place of *or* is limiting and that, through the power of *and*, we are liberated. Maybe you'll choose to embrace the fact that we are all vessels for God's work or that when living in flow, life is easy, you see results, and you have fun.

I am not going to tell you the process of transformation is easy. You don't just snap your fingers and become able to integrate, face your shadow, have compassion, alter the way you think, and reach your defining moment overnight. The tools of transformation require repetitive use and constant practice. That said, reaching your defining moment does not happen on a linear timeline either. It's not like training for a marathon, where you start at one mile, and over the course of twenty weeks, you build up to your twenty-mile training run. There is the ability to start and evolve quickly. For some of you, you may advance through your transformation with ease and speed. For others of you, you may have to work at it a bit more. Regardless, no matter how long it takes, with every ounce of application and fortitude, your neural pathways will begin to rewire. You will biologically and spiritually evolve. No matter what, you will always be moving in the right direction, and every step along your journey will be worth it.

Please accept that you have a purpose. Know that you are being called. For those of you still residing in your known world with your journey into the unknown lying in wait, there is so much more for you. The key to coming to know your purpose is to quiet your mind and get to a place in your life where you can hear the phone ringing three rooms down. It comes when you still your thoughts enough to intuit your summons. When you hear the faint tone, walk down the hallway, barge through the door, and answer the call.

Embark on your journey. Apply action and fortitude, so you can move through your abyss and transformation with grace. Know you are the hero and that you do not have to go to a synagogue, a church, or a mosque in order to reach your defining moment. You don't have to move to an ashram or sit on a meditation pillow all day. All you need is within you. You are divine. You can and should have it all.

May your path be clear and may you inspire others on your way. Through your contributions and a commitment to heeding your call and fulfilling your journey, you will repair the world.

MANIFESTO

"You are what your deep, driving desire is.
As your desire is, so is your will. As your will is,
so is your deed. As your deed is, so is your destiny."

—Brihadaranyaka Upanishad

You have been invited to heed your call, and now it is up to you to decide where you go from here. You are the result of the choices you make every single day, and what you choose, you become. To choose wisely, be a witness to your thoughts and actions, both positive and negative. Observe each and every one with neutral emotion. Avoid judging or being critical. Just examine your thoughts as they pass through your psyche. Consider the source, then act or don't act on them. How you choose to respond to this call is what will define and shape your future.

Move through life with awareness. When you proceed with action, be aware of your intentions and the origin of your actions. Are you living from a place of fear or scarcity? Are you engaging life from a place of needing to be seen, validated, or heard? Consider these things as you move through each day and do so by listening to your inner voice. It will tell you what you need and what is true for you. Your intuition will guide you and will not lead you astray. It is only when you rush from place to place, when you allow yourself to become distracted by your devices and ego, that you lose your way.

It is likely you have had many thoughts while reading this book. They may have sounded something like, *I can't live a life like this. I don't have time to slow down and be present. My life is too demanding. I can't just go with the flow.* Maybe you've considered that you *can* live a more purposeful and mindful life, but aren't ready right now, and that you intend to live more mindfully starting next month. Do not judge these thoughts; do not banish them. Instead, observe them from a place of neutrality, and say to yourself, "I am the silent ever present witness of my thoughts, feelings, and emotions, and I can choose how I will use them." As you practice neutrality and witnessing awareness, you will begin to form the habit of mindful living. You will learn what is best for you and how to live the life that best supports your unique journey. Your stories and tales from your past will not own you, and you'll be better able to do what fulfills you, what drives you and inspires you to live a joyful and abundant life.

When you become more centered, you'll be able to create opportunities that will support a life of ease, a life with more joy, and one that blesses you with the results you desire. Be relentless in the pursuit of choosing what serves you in the highest and best way. As Rumi says, "Respond to every call that excites your spirit." As you do, you will write the story of your future. You will fulfill your journey and as a result will help heal the world.

Tokens of Lifestyle Wisdom

To help you in heeding your call, following are some lifestyle choices, tools, and practices for authentic and joyful living that I've found to be useful in my own journey.

1. *Your life is precious.* To honor your existence, cultivate an attitude of gratitude. Appreciate your every breath and the unique gifts you've been blessed with. Savor every moment, the highs and the lows. The highs are meant for you to celebrate, and the lows help you learn and grow.

2. *Love more.* Most of all, love your spirit and your body. Thank your body for showing up for you every single day. For your heart beating and your lungs breathing without any calls from you to do so. Your body is a magnificent machine and never complains unless you abuse it. So please don't abuse it. You truly do only get one, and it deserves to be respected and nurtured. Turn that love outward. Let your smile shine. Smile at the barista who makes your coffee each morning. Ask them how their day is going. Enroll them in conversation. Smile at the grocery store clerk, at your neighbor, your staff, and co-workers. Make a habit of inviting someone else to feel special each day. Smile with your eyes. Let light shine through you to touch the life of someone else.

3. *Listen intently.* Don't just hear what another is saying, but observe their body language to tune into their unspoken words. This is how you build empathy. This is how you cultivate intuition. Listen with not only your ears, but also your heart. Feel the *why* behind another sharing their life with you. Consider what you can share with them in return to encourage, support, or uplift.

4. *Embrace your inner child.* Goof off. Skip. Laugh more. Boogie if you feel like it. Try being childlike at least once each day. Next time you eat gelato, ice cream, a cookie, or a new food you have never tried, really taste it. Be mindful and savor every last bite. Get outside and play. Go for a hike; read a book in the yard; splash in rain puddles. What's the worst that can happen? You get a little

wet or dirty . . . It's good for you. It awakens you to the moment, and you will feel more alive.

5. *Don't hold back.* When you have a heart-centered desire, don't cage it. Go for it instead, and pour all your intention into the mission. Don't tell yourself you're not good enough, *or* it's not possible, *or* your idea is silly. Be unapologetically driven to achieve your desired life. See the world as one big opportunity and manifest. Go and pull a snake from the grass if you believe one is there for the taking.

6. *Be a warrior for peace.* Instead of arguing, diffuse a fight. Instead of engaging in confrontation, proceed with compassion. Instead of promoting violence, practice restraint. Pause before retorting. Literally count to ten if you need to in order to gain clarity in a situation. Extend peace to the driver who cuts you off. Breath while waiting in a lengthy line rather than huffing and puffing and tapping your feet.

7. *Be mighty; act humbly.* Believe in your greatness, and at the same time, practice humility. Know that *ruach*, God's breath, is flowing through you. You are not the only one orchestrating your life. You are co-creating with all consciousness, with the universe, and with source. Let this humble and empower you.

8. *Practice unsolicited kindness.* Hold the door for someone and then just keep holding it for others. Pay it forward by plugging a meter other than your own. Let someone else go in front of you at the bank or the grocery store. Over tip. Send a note of love and appreciation to a new person each day, whether an extended family member, an employee, a friend, a co-worker, or someone who provides services to you.

9. *Connect with nature.* Step outside in the morning and take a deep breath of fresh air. Look up at the sky at least twice a day, and consider the wonders of the world. Let the wind rush over you, and allow it to guide you. Listen to the pitter patter of raindrops on your roof. Watch autumn leaves fall silently to the earth. Play in the snow. Take a walk around a park, a hike through the forest, or stroll on the beach.

10. *Practice mindfulness.* Prior to making a purchase, really consider the brand you are supporting. Consider what they represent and how that purchase will affect others around the globe. Pause before you eat. Pay attention to the food choices you make. Consider why you choose to eat the foods you do and how you can be more mindful and make better eating choices. Avoid distraction while eating. Chew thoroughly, and be grateful for the meal.

11. *Be present.* Before picking up your phone to text, post, pin, or tweet, stop and consider why you're choosing to connect digitally. Is it to run away from your emotions? Is it to distract you from your state of being? Is it a means to gain attention and be noticed? Be mindful of how often you connect with your devices rather than connecting with yourself and others.

Access Your Natural Pharmacy

The following is a list of natural modalities that help in accessing the body's natural pharmacy and promoting well-being.

1. *Healing sounds.* Listen to calming music, the sounds of nature, chanting, or children laughing. Turn on music that helps you relax. Turn off any that promotes stress and anxiety.

2. *Healing touch.* Treat yourself to a massage. Buy a dry brush, and brush your skin from the souls of your feet to your chin. This activity stimulates blood flow, detoxifies, and feels incredible. Give yourself an oil massage each day after you shower. Spend five minutes rubbing sunflower, sweet almond, sesame, olive, or coconut oil into every inch of your skin. It's nourishing and most importantly, the action shows loving kindness to yourself, making you more likely to show love to others.

3. *Healing taste.* Eat food that is whole and seasonal. Avoid foods that are processed or contain artificial ingredients. Buy locally and organic whenever possible. Eat foods that are vibrant and colorful. Taste and savor every bite. Consider the energy of the sun that helped produce natural foods, and feel that energy being absorbed into your body. Chew slowly. Cook at home as much as possible and cook with friends and family. When you sit down to your evening meal, light candles, open a nice bottle of wine, or turn on soothing music. Make this meal special. Let twelve hours pass from your evening meal to breakfast so your body can properly digests the day's food.

4. *Healing smell.* Add aromatherapy and candles to your home. Select those that evoke a sense of calm, relaxation, purification, or energy. Burn incense. Buy naturally scented soaps, candles, and oils. In cooler months, light a fire and inhale the aroma of burning wood.

5. *Reflect upon your day.* Before going to sleep, spend five minutes quietly letting your day (from when you woke up to the present) play across your mind like you were watching a movie. Try not to attach to any part of your day—just witness and review. Then, silently ask your self three questions: (1) Who am I? (2) What do

I want? (3) What is the purpose of my life? Simply release these questions into the universe. Do not try to answer them. Then, silently say to yourself, "I wish to remember my dreams." Keep a pen and journal near your bed so that you can write down your dreams as soon as you open your eyes the following morning. Pay attention to whether answers to those three questions come to you in your dreams. Study characters and animals that visit you in your dreams.

6. *Power off.* For at least thirty minutes each day, perhaps at night or first thing in the morning, disconnect completely and embrace silence. Avoid writing, reading, watching TV, or connecting with your computer, iPad, or smartphone. Quiet your thoughts and embrace silence. Silence is the language of God. When you are silent, you can better experience the voice of your soul, and it will be easier to heed your call.

7. *Meditate.* Sit quietly with your eyes closed, focusing on nothing but your breath. As thoughts come, observe them. Do not judge them and then let them go by coming back to the awareness of your breathing. Do this every single day for a minimum of five minutes and for up to sixty minutes or even more if you choose to. Cultivate that calm, centered state of being throughout your day. Be meditative in all actions.

8. *Heed your call!* Do what you love, and do it now. This is your life! If it's not easy, if you are not having fun, if you are not getting the results you want, then stop. If you are pushing a headwind, turn around and proceed in the other direction. If you feel you don't have enough time to heed your call, reduce the amount of time you spend on social media. Turn off the television, and stop surfing the web. You'll have more time than you ever imagined. If

you are worried about not knowing what your calling is, don't be; it will find you if you ask for it to be discovered. Be open to new ways of thinking and to unexplored opportunities.

What to Expect

When you heed your call, you will go forth with more ease. You'll experience more harmony and peace in your life. You will have more time for activities you enjoy and will feel less anxious and stressed. You will come to trust your instincts more, and when chaos presents itself, you'll seem to glide through the situation less affected. You'll experience an increase in energy and creativity. You may even stimulate your libido. Chances are, you'll feel lighter and more vibrant and will likely glow from the inside out. Your eyes will be brighter, clearer, and sparklier.

You will attract relationships that are mutually beneficial, rich, and unconditionally loving. You'll manifest your desires more effortlessly. Time will cease to be linear, and you'll accomplish more than ever before. You'll attract like-minded, inspiring friends, co-workers, staff, and lovers. You will become more empathetic and intuitive. You will no longer be afraid of being alone and will feel comfortable in your own company, even without your devices that connect you to the outside world. You will make friends with your shadow and as a result, will become aware of your power and energy. You will see the world as more than just right and wrong, black and white, this camp or the other. You'll recognize there is only one camp. Your work will no longer feel like work—in fact, it will become hard to distinguish between work, play, and life because you'll discover they are all one.

You will be aligned with your core values and higher purpose. Your world will become richer, more Technicolor, more beautiful. You'll be inspired to create. You'll embrace hardships and challenges because you'll know they serve as your mentors and guides; they serve to teach you and help you grow. You'll take leaps of faith because you'll know the journey ahead is richer than the known world you've left behind. Synchronicities will abound. Miracles will happen daily. You will no longer feel the need to seek validation. You will come to believe in yourself, and that alone will be enough.

You will sleep soundly like a child who has been playing all day. You will be so focused on the present moment that time will cease to feel linear. The weight you have been struggling to lose will drop off, and you will naturally become your ideal weight. Vices and energy-decreasing habits will be reduced, if not disappear, and they will be replaced with life-affirming habits and lifestyle choices. Money will flow to you with ease. You will experience abundance, and you'll feel joy in being able to share it with others.

I share this message with you as encouragement to actively engage in your journey and to suggest what is possible. Yes, you still need to put on your shoes and head out for the run. Yes, you still have to choose whether or not you want to answer the phone ringing three rooms down. No one can take the journey for you. It is up to you to engage. By my writing this book and sharing this message, I'm inviting you to heed your call and to be a hero of your own life. I'm enrolling you in the possibility of achieving your heart-centered desires. You now have the tools to do so. And when you participate in the life-affirming activities previously outlined, not only will you be building an abundant and joyful life for yourself, you also will be participating in the invention of a better future for all of humanity. You will be doing your part to repair not only your experience and future, but also that of the world.

Appendix A

THE ELEMENTS OF HEEDING YOUR CALL

Known World

The patterns and programming of our youth. The comfortable job that we are at but that is not fulfilling. The relationship we're in that satisfies our desire for socioeconomic status and companionship, yet does not feed our soul. This is where the phone is ringing, but perhaps our ears are not yet attuned, or we are deliberating choosing not to answer, choosing not to heed our call.

Unknown World

We embark into our unknown world when we take a leap of faith and accept our unique summons. Once in the unknown world, we experience somewhat short-lived feelings of elation and joy because we are finally free of the demands, habits, and programs of our known world. We inevitably do not ride this initial high forever because there are important lessons to be learned that will help us reach our defining moment. The feelings of elation are replaced with feelings of despair or a feeling of having gotten lost on our path, and we fall then into our abyss.

Abyss

In the abyss, we may feel hopeless, confused, or fear we made the wrong decision. We may feel insecure about our ability to keep up with our new role or our calling. Perhaps we don't feel good enough, worthy, or capable. Perhaps we don't feel the path we are on is the right one for us. We invariably experience these emotions as they prepare us to meet our mentors and guides. These teachers can then support us in ascending from our chasm of uncertainty and continue on our journey.

Guides and Mentors

Like Dorothy meeting the Tin Man and Luke being guided by Yoda and Obi-Wan Kenobi, we come to know our mentors and guides. Sometimes they are teachers in our social groups, and sometimes they are peers. Often times, however, they are our shadow parts, those qualities we try to bury and hide that we deem negative or appalling. These shadow qualities are instructive and important to embrace. They teach us that all characteristics, the ugly and beautiful, the impatient and accommodating, serve a purpose and support us in our journeys. Once we accept our totality, we are ready to receive and implement our tools for transformation. In my experience, there are eleven that have served to be the most valuable in my journey and that of those I work with and advise.

Tools for Transformation

Empathy

We are each born with the gift of empathy. Some of us have been able to develop this deep level of compassion more than others, but it can be cultivated by anyone with applied attention to the task. When we call on empathy and infuse this tool into our interactions, we are better able to arrive at mutual wins. As we step into the shoes of another, we are able to see more clearly where they are coming from. As a result, we are more efficient at finding solutions. Perhaps because we have been there ourselves or perhaps by having compassion for their situation while not directly experiencing it ourselves, we can more clearly see a way out.

Co-Creation

We alone do not create our future. Our individual thoughts and actions impact our experiences of tomorrow, but it is our collective creation, our co-creation with God, source, and the universe, that writes the stories of our lives. Like my son Sawyer believing with his whole heart he would find a snake in the grass and then did, we too can achieve our wildest dreams if we expand our view of possibility to one that is infinite.

Conscious Communication

We are evolving and so too should our speech and interactions. Words and phrases like *sustainable* and *work-life balance* need to be replaced with more universally aligned words, phrases, and terminology. To live sustainably is limiting. *Work-life balance* connotes separation. It says there is life and then there is work, and this is simply not true. There is just life. Similarly, the term *mind, body, spirit connection* suggests there is separation between them when there is not. We are simply whole beings.

Invoking Archetypes

Archetypes are not just notable characters in mythological and religious stories. They are instructive energies, whose qualities, if we choose to invoke them, can help us be more mindful in our relationships with others and ourselves. As an example, if we feel insecurity about leaving our comfort zone, we may want to invoke the qualities of the Archangel Michael who represents strength and courage or perhaps the Cowardly Lion in *The Wizard of Oz*.

If it is creativity and innovation we seek to bring into our business experience, perhaps we should invoke the qualities of Merlin, the wizard who can manifest outcomes that wouldn't otherwise occur under familiar laws of nature.

Most of all, knowing what archetypes we most resonate with is important, as from there, we can best know which ones to invoke at any given time.

The Power of And (Integration)

There is significant value in embracing integration. When we consciously choose to blend artistry with skill, intuition with fact, and purpose with process, we address life holistically. When we unite "left-brain" qualities most frequently experienced in life and business with those that are softer and more traditionally "right brain," we build harmonious bonds of qualities that reveal sound solutions and promote positive outcomes.

Manifestation

We are manifesting all the time by the content of our thoughts. Our thoughts and desires literally become things, and as a result, what we attract may either be positive or negative. Manifestation does not consider can't, don't, and not; it only responds to the subject matter of our thoughts. It is important then for us not to give energy to negative thoughts. If we don't want clients whose payments are late, we should seek clients who pay on time. If we don't want staff who is pessimistic, we should request employees who take initiative—those who are motivated by finding solutions rather than re-hashing what isn't working.

Surrender

We should avoid forcing agreements, timing, and outcomes. Again, because our thoughts shape our future, if we focus too intently on a particular outcome, we may attract what is ultimately not in our best interest. The tool of surrender reminds us that when we put a positive intention into the collective unconscious, and then let go, we open ourselves up to infinite possibility. We cannot foresee the future and though we may think we know what is best for our lives, we truly can't know for sure. Surrender means having a belief in unseen possibilities.

Living in Flow

In order to proceed through our journey with ease, it is best to be flexible with the manifestation of our desires. We should set intentions; we should put on our shoes and set out for our run, but be willing to head in the direction where the wind will be at our back. If we let the universe guide us and do not resist, we will actualize our greatness. Similarly, we should not hoard our love, gifts, or desires, as to do so suffocates and limits our potential.

Humility

We are flutes through which God's breath blows. We have each been blessed with various gifts and are vessels for delivering these gifts to the world. We are co-creating our lives all the time and should recognize we have been empowered to do so, but alone do not manifest our lives. When we remain humble and cultivate gratitude for every gift, every convenience of life, every blessing, and experience, we receive more of the same.

Embracing Your Shadow

The world is a mirror and those we interact with are our reflection. By recognizing a quality in another, we too embody that characteristic. Our ego and spirit consist of a mash up of traits: those we deem to be unacceptable and negative and those we recognize as attractive and honorable. As such, we each have the capacity to be a bitchy, arrogant, boisterous, rude, or inconsiderate. We are also all capable of being inspiring, loving, gracious, poised, and courteous. When we come to accept and honor our totality, we are better able to ascertain the life we desire because we are no longer bound by our shadow parts, the ones that when not accepted, wreck havoc on our lives in dark and mysterious ways.

Accepting Our Unity

The vibration of our thoughts and actions affect all of humanity. By heeding our call and manifesting our heart-centered desires, we create vibrations of happiness, joy, and gratitude. These vibrations ripple out into the world and are experienced by others. In turn, they feel positively affected and are more inclined to act and speak in ways that maintain that high vibration. It is important for us then to be mindful of our thoughts and actions, as they quite literally shape our future one vibration at a time.

Appendix B

ACCESSING ARCHETYPAL ENERGIES

The word *archetype* comes from the Greek *arkhetypos*, meaning "first imprint." The term was originally meant to define the model upon which something is based. In Plato's "Theory of Forms," which first introduced the idea of archetypes, the term was used to describe objects, as opposed to how it is typically used today. Swiss psychiatrist Carl Jung popularized the term as it is typically used now, and is used throughout this book, to shed light on personality through universal forms that are models of behavior.

Lists of archetypes have grown in length as time has gone on with some lists starting at twelve archetypes and growing all the way to over thirty, though some people argue that a list of archetypes is futile because the possibilities are endless. That being said, many people in the field of psychology and philosophy have, since Jung introduced the idea, expanded upon and tweaked the idea of archetypes, often defining and delineating new and different categories.

Some notable authors and scholars who have used and defined archetypes are Caroline Myss, Clarissa Pinkola-Estes, Robert A. Johnson, and, of course, Joseph Campbell. For our purposes, we will look at the eight archetypes discussed in the Hero's Journey, and you can refer to this list in order to invoke more of each archetypes' qualities. Clearly, this is not an exhaustive list, so feel free to explore other lists and other archetypes when you are ready to call for more or different qualities.

With that being said, this list is a wonderful place to start. As archetypes are patterns of behavior, symbolized by standard types of characters in movies and stories, you can also look to books, films, and other forms of entertainment to find archetypes to call on.

HEROES

The hero is, of course, the central figure in a story, the protagonist, the one that we root for and whose calling is to sacrifice him- or herself and to leave the known word to complete a journey. Typically, the hero suffers through separation for the greater good.

There are a number of different types of heroes within this archetype: the willing hero, the reluctant hero, the innocent hero, the wandering hero, and the list goes on and on. The important thing to remember is that when it comes right down to it, everyone is the hero of his or her own story, so the hero you invoke can be any type of hero you can envision. The essence of the hero is the sacrifice, so that should be kept in mind when invoking the hero archetype, no matter what type of hero one invokes.

Some well-known heroes are: Frodo, Luke Skywalker, Neo (*The Matrix*), William Wallace (*Braveheart*), Jesus, Wonder Woman, Harry Potter, King Arthur (*Le Mort d'Arthur*), Simba (*The Lion King*), Dorothy (*The Wizard of Oz*), Joan of Arc, Superman, and Buffy Summers (*Buffy the Vampire Slayer*).

SHADOWS

Shadows are traditionally portrayed as villains and enemies, sometimes even as the enemy within a hero, instead of a separate character (much like our own shadows). The shadow represents that which we want to typically push down and hide, what we want to pretend isn't there. The shadow is always a worthy opponent, though it is not always a bad person; often it is simply someone whose goals are in opposition to the hero's.

Because what we deny will chase us, and when we repress things, they can become dangerous without an outlet, it is important to accept this side of ourselves and invoke these qualities at times. The shadow can be as simple as the dark side of the Force or even the repressed possibilities of the hero. For these purposes, it is often easier to think of the shadow as a character.

When invoking the shadow archetype, picking a shadow character that also has good qualities that can readily be seen is often the most effective choice, such as Professor Snape (*Harry Potter* series), the Wicked Witch of the West (*Wizard of Oz*), Lex Luthor (*Superman*), Darth Vader (*Star Wars*), Faith (*Buffy the Vampire Slayer*), Tyler Durden (*Fight Club*), and Catwoman (*Batman*).

Others may be invoked simply because you feel it's time to embrace darkness and power, so other villains can be invoked as well, such as: Sauron (*The Lord of the Ring*s trilogy), Iago (*Othello*), Cruella de Vil (*One Hundred and One Dalmations*), the Joker, Voldemort (*Harry Potter* series), Grendel (*Beowulf*), etc.

MENTORS

The mentor archetype is the hero's guide or guiding principles and can be met at any point during the journey. The mentor archetype provides motivation, wisdom, and training to the hero—this can be done by a mentor who is intentionally wise and purposefully teaching the hero or by a mentor who is a fool and is unknowingly helping the hero by teaching lessons that are specific to the journey.

When invoking a mentor, it is typically better to invoke an intentional mentor, since the foolish ones, though they serve us well on our journeys, probably will not have the specific qualities we are searching for. We can actually think of mentors in our own lives by bringing to mind a teacher or coach who inspired us and meant a lot to us.

If we look to classic film, literature, and other cultural stories, we can find mentors as well, like Yoda, Merlin, Obi-Wan Kenobi, Gandalf, Glinda the Good Witch (*The Wizard of Oz*), Athena, Rupert Giles (*Buffy the Vampire Slayer*), Dumbledore (*Harry Potter* series), Professor Xavier (*X-Men*), the fairy godmother (*Cinderella*), and Q (*James Bond*).

HERALD

The herald is an important archetype because he or she issues the call to adventure. In stories, the herald can be a person, an event, or a force of some kind. Basically, the herald upsets the equilibrium and sets the hero on his adventure, so if you're feeling like you're stagnating or need something to bring about change, it may be time to invoke a herald archetype.

Obviously, it can be difficult to focus on an event or force in this capacity, but here's a list of famous heralds that can get you looking in the right direction to hear (and heed) a new call: Hagrid (*Harry Potter* series), Gandalf, Mr. Poe (*A Series of Unfortunate Events*), the Silver Surfer, R2D2 (*Star Wars*), Ford Prefect (*The Hitchhiker's Guide to the Galaxy*), Effe Trinket (*The Hunger Games*), and John the Baptist.

THRESHOLD GUARDIANS

These archetypes are pretty well defined by their name: they are the forces that stand in the way at important turning points. These can be jealous enemies, literal gatekeepers, or the hero's own fears and doubts. These guardians test the hero's courage and stamina by protecting the secrets of the unknown world, which requires the hero to prove his or her commitment.

Usually, this archetype is encountered early in our journeys, as the guardian also shows us that our journey will not be easy and so prepares us for what is to come. We may want to invoke this archetype when we want to be privy to the secrets of the unknown, when we want to be challenged and show our bravery and commitment.

Some threshold guardians out there are the Cowardly Lion, Draco Malfoy (*Harry Potter* series), Cordelia Chase (first season of *Buffy the Vampire Slayer*), the sphinx, the many people encountered by the Knights of the Round Table, Uncle Ben and Han Solo (*Star Wars*), Little John (*Robin Hood*), and Inigo and Fezzig (*The Princess Bride*).

SHAPESHIFTERS

In stories, shapeshifters can be literal creatures that shapeshift, like vampires or werewolves, and they represent change—our own changes, the way other people change, and the constant changing of the world's circumstances. The shapeshifter's initial shape is often misleading to the hero because he hides his true nature and makes his loyalties and endgame unclear. His very changeability keeps the hero on his toes and guessing.

Many times in story, the shapeshifter is someone of the opposite sex who remains unclear to the hero and who is often a catalyst for changing the hero's journey, outlook, or personality, causing them to question their current beliefs or assumptions. Mentors can appear as shapeshifters as well, but it's wonderful for these purposes to think of a specific shapeshifter who has the qualities that you are currently wanting to embrace. When we want to embrace our own mysteriousness and challenge our current perspective, we should look to these shapeshifters.

Some shapeshifters that may be familiar to you are Mystique (*The X-Men*), Princess Leia (*Star Wars*), the Chesire Cat (*Alice in Wonderland*), Angel (*Buffy the Vampire Slayer*), Gollum (*Lord of the Rings* trilogy), the Wizard (*The Wizard of Oz*), Zeus, and Sylar (*Heroes*).

TRICKSTERS

The trickster archetype is made up of mischief makers, who mirror our own mischievous subconscious and urge us to change. They relish disrupting the status quo and providing comic relief. They often help the hero by making sure that they do not get too big of an ego or begin to think they can do no wrong. Typically, they enjoy a bit of chaos and bring it into the Hero's Journey by questioning and mocking the current state of affairs.

When we're starting to take things too seriously and accept things as they are too often, it's important that we take note and call on the trickster archetype. By embracing our prankster and mischievous side, we remember to keep things light and that nothing is so serious that we can't get past it. When we need a little laughter and absurdity, it's time to call on the trickster.

Some famous tricksters are Loki (from Norse mythology), Groucho Marx, the cat (*The Cat in the Hat*), Fred and George Weasley (*Harry Potter* series), Puck (*A Midsummer Night's Dream*), Han Solo, the Native American coyote, Spike (*Buffy the Vampire Slayer*), the Mad Hatter (*Alice in Wonderland*), Spider-Man, and Merry and Pippin (*The Lord of the Rings* trilogy).

Appendix C

ADAPTING THE HERO'S JOURNEY

Throughout *Heed Your Call*, we've used the general stages of Joseph Campbell's Hero's Journey to help illustrate each of our own journeys through work and life. The work we do at Meriwether Group is what we call "The Founder's Journey" and is based on his monomyth as well.

His work underpins the main points of the Meriwether Group's quite well, and Campbell identified seventeen steps that make up the Hero's Journey. While very few myths contain all of these steps, and these steps may be organized in a number of ways, knowing them all can be helpful in your journey.

The Seventeen Stages of Joseph Campbell's Monomyth

Departure
- The Call to Adventure
- Refusal of the Call

- Supernatural Aid
- The Crossing of the First Threshold
- Belly of the Whale

Initiation
- The Road of Trials
- The Meeting with the Goddess
- Woman as Temptress
- Atonement with the Father
- Apotheosis
- The Ultimate Boon

Return
- Refusal of the Return
- The Magic Flight
- Rescue from Without
- The Crossing of the Return Threshold
- Master of Two Worlds
- Freedom to Live

The journey we've outlined in this book is not the first time this monomyth has been adapted. Phil Cousineau, who considered Campbell a mentor, wrote *The Hero's Journey: A Biographical Portrait*, a documentary film about Campbell's life. The film led Cousineau to write the book *The Hero's Journey: Joseph Campbell on His Life and World*, and he was later inspired from this work to modernize and consolidate these following steps.

The Eight Stages of Cousineau's Hero's Journey

- The Call to Adventure
- The Road of Trials

- The Vision Quest
- The Meeting with the Goddess
- The Boon
- The Magic Flight
- The Return Threshold
- The Master of Two Worlds

Another eight-step consolidation was done by David Adams Leeming in his book *Mythology: The Voyage of the Hero*, an anthology that collects a wide array of narrative texts to illustrate how myths help us in our universal search for meaning.

The Eight Stages of Leeming's Hero's Journey

- Miraculous Conception and Birth
- Initiation of the Hero-child
- Withdrawal from Family or Community for Meditation and Preparation
- Trial and Quest
- Death (real or symbolic)
- Descent into the Underworld
- Resurrection and Rebirth
- Ascension, Apotheosis, and Atonement

Which brings us to the Hero's Journey we cover here, based on the Founder's Journey:

The Call
Crossing the Threshold
The Abyss
- Revelations
- Meet with Mentor

The Transformation
- Trust
- Surrender
- Empathy
- Living in Flow
- The Power of Co-Creation
- Empowerment
- Embracing your Shadow
- Integration/the Power of *And*
- Invoking your Archetypes
- Universal Message
- Universal Connectedness

Defining Moment
Fulfillment & Giving Back

Though these are the most well-known iterations of the Hero's Journey, it's important to remember that the journey is cyclical. We can be on any number of journeys at a time, so we may be encountering these steps at different times, in different orders, or maybe not even reaching certain points along our journey. These are meant to give us a general outline of the journey we may be on currently, but we shouldn't feel like these are rigid and are the only way to experience our journeys. The more we understand our journeys, the better equipped we are to heed our calls!

ACKNOWLEDGMENTS

JFK airport—an unlikely oasis of calm after an exhaustive and productive week of business meetings with Modern-day Heroes. I am wrapping up the trip seated in the airport's business class lounge, sipping on sparkling water with lime. My feet are elevated, and I'm typing wildly on my iPhone attempting to get out all that is in my heart right now.

Despite missing my family and feeling beat up from traffic jams, delayed flights, late night imbibing, one too many heavy meals, and cranky cabbies, I'm smiling ear to ear, grinning while I reflect on the many meetings I just held with entrepreneurs—warrior spirits who are heeding their calls, those who have stepped foot or are about to embark into the unknown world of commerce. Together, we have laughed, we've cried, we've set intentions, and we've examined challenges they may encounter along the way. Though completely wiped out, I feel connected, joyful, and inspired.

ACKNOWLEDGMENTS

As I write, I am overwhelmed with appreciation not only for those I met this week, but also for everyone and everything that has ever inspired me. I am beyond grateful for those who have believed in me and supported my journey through the known and unknown worlds. I am grateful even for those who I perceived as hindrances in my path and for challenges and heartache—they too were necessary for me to evolve. While I sit here waiting for my delayed flight, I'm seizing the opportunity to acknowledge all who have made this book possible.

First, God, source, the universe, Mohammed, Buddha, the collective consciousness, thank you for this great life—all of it. Thank you for gifting me my unique journey and dharma. It is beyond what I could have ever imagined for myself.

Thank you, family—Dad, Mom, Dan, Jonathan, Kelly, Jenny, Bill, Lena, Al, Miriam, Joe, Uncle Harvey, and Gary—thank you for both your dark and light shadows, for the suffering I was subject to and for the endless love. It is you who have tested *and* exalted my soul with your endless love. You have influenced and molded my journey.

Thank you, Heather, for your inspiring and child-like spirit, for your vata energy, and for your way of living that has taught me many of life's great lessons. In the near two decades of our marriage, you've taught me about manifestation and about how to live in the moment. You've taught me to proceed with love and how to chill out. Thank you for showing my soul how to rest and just be.

Sawyer and Hailey, my sweet angels, you routinely show me the universe. Your eyes sparkle with purity, beauty, art, love, and purpose. Your innocence and youthful enthusiasm show me how to be one with possibility. Thank you.

Tina Leigh, thank you for getting inside my brain, for taking my endless stream of thoughts and transforming them into this beautiful and inspiring story. Thank you for believing in me and reminding me all I ever need to do is trust—trust source to flow through me to you, like breath through a flute. I feel held and our journeys are now forever connected. This work would have never manifested had it not been for you.

Bo Rinaldi, thank you for building a strong foundation for me to stand on, a platform from which I could launch. Thank you for holding space and validating my impulses to do this work. I feel understood and appreciated. You've helped me feel that this book and I are important and valuable.

To my personal friends, teachers at Denison, Lewis and Clark, and in life—a few of them being: the Friedmans, Julie B., Fogger, Bill N., Wedds, Scott S., Nita, Naomi, Coach Haney, Keith M., Ken B., Craig J., JagatJoti, Durg, Knacker, Wiens, Hoek, Kubes, Gewey, Blake, Court, Nic, Bill, Coach, Roegs, Brauner, Rick J., Curt M., Butch, Dale R., Anna P., and James H.—as well as business partners and staff at the Meriwether Group—thank you for your insights, inspiration, humor, gifts, and talents. You've blessed my life immensely. You truly serve the hero every day and do so with grace, honor, expertise, and a hell of a lot of fun. Thank you for your support and for sharing your individual journeys with me.

To Mary, my turtle, you constantly have my back, know what I need before I need it, are my second set of eyes and ears, and you bring heart, brains and courage to MWG and me every day. You have held me up and allowed me to truly heed my call and continue on my journey even when doing so seemed impossible. Thank you.

Joseph Campbell, I wish you were walking the earth today, man. You are one of my greatest sources of inspiration. Thank you for your powerful insights into our very existence, for crafting *The Hero's Journey* and sharing it with the world.

Deepak and all teachers, mentors, and guides at the Chopra Center, you've opened my eyes to my soul. You've guided me through my process of transformation and gifted me essential tools that have been, and continue to be, useful in my transformation.

To all of the great thinkers, teachers, and bearers of light who have blessed this planet with wisdom, service, innovation, and creativity, thank you.

Dan Pink, your work has been hugely influential in the development of our Meriwether ethos. Thank you for being a vessel for such powerful and instructive insights on integration.

To each and every client of Meriwether Group, thank you for trusting and allowing us to support you in your journey. Jay, Dave, Richard, Jane and Doug, Franz, Leo, Kaie, Cat Daddy, Tres, Mort, Justin, Kade, Duane, Susan, and David, serving you has allowed me to live out my dharma, and for that I am deeply grateful.

And lastly, to all heroes around the globe, to all of you who are on your journey and those of you still in the known world but at least listening, even occasionally, to your summons, thank you for attuning your ears to what is possible for you. You inspire all those around you. You inspire me. In deepest gratitude to all, thank you.

NOTES

Introduction

1. Joseph Campbell, *The Hero with a Thousand Faces* (New York: New World Library, 2008), 15.

Part I

Chapter 1

1. George Lucas, "The Mythology of Star Wars with George Lucas and Bill Moyers," *BillMoyers.com* Vimeo, 1999 (filmed), http://vimeo.com/38026023.

Chapter 2

1. Chuck Palahniuk, *Fight Club* (New York: Norton & Company, 2005), 17.

2. Ibid, 59.

Chapter 3

1. Campbell, *Hero with a Thousand Faces*.

2. Consciousness: The Web Course, "Lecture 10. Consciousness and Emotion," (pdf, The Center for Consciousness Studies, September 23, 2013), http://bernardbaars .pbworks.com/f/Lect10_Emotions+.pdf.

3. Carl Gustav Jung, *"The Shadow,"* Psychologist Anywhere Anytime, September 1, 2013 (last accessed), http://www.psychologistanywhereanytime.com/famous_psychologist _and_psychologists/psychologist_famous_carl_jung.htm.

4. Chip Hartranft, *The Yoga-Sutra of Patanjali: A New Translation with Commentary* (Boston, MA: Shambala Press, 2003).

5. Debbie Ford, *The Dark Side of the Light Chasers* (New York, NY: Riverhead Books, 1998), 11.

6. Daniel M. Wegner, "The Art and Science of Thought Suppression," (PowerPoint presentation, Harvard University, May 2013), slides 9-11, http://contextualscience.org /system/files/Art_and_Science_of_Thought_Suppression_compressed.pdf.

7. J. R. R. Tolkien, *The Fellowship of the Ring* (Boston: Mariner Books, 1999).

8. Deepak Chopra, "Seduction of Spirit Retreat," The Chopra Center, Carlsbad, CA, August 23–29, 2009.

9. Deepak Chopra, Debbie Ford, and Marianne Williamson, *The Shadow Effect* (New York, NY: HarperOne, 2010), 80.

10. Friedrich Nietzsche, *Thus Spake Zarathustra: Part I, Zarathustra's Prologue,* trans. Thomas Common (Project Gutenberg, 2008): http://www.gutenberg.org/files/1998/1998 -h/1998-h.htm.

11. Ford, *The Dark Side of The Light Chasers,* 110–111.

12. *The I Ching or Book of Changes,* trans. Hellmut Wilhelm (New Jersey: Princeton University Press, 1977).

Chapter 4

1. Dean Radin, "Superpowers and the Stubborn Illusion of Separation," *Subtle Energies and Energy Medicine,* 19, no 1(2008): 29–42, http://journals.sfu.ca/seemj/index.php/ seemj/article/view/411/372.

2. Jeffrey Bub, "Quantum Entanglement and Information," *The Stanford Encyclopedia of Philosophy* (Winter 2010 Edition), Edward N. Zalta (ed.), http://plato.stanford.edu /archives/win2010/entries/qt-entangle/.

3. "Quantum Entanglement," *Science Daily*, accessed September 19, 2013, http://www .sciencedaily.com/articles/q/quantum_entanglement.htm.

4. Remy Melina, "Are We Really All Made of Stars?" *Live Science*, October 13, 2010, http://www.livescience.com/32828-humans-really-made-stars.html.

5. Michael Loewenstein and Amy Fredericks on Carl Sagan, "Ask An Astrophysicist," NASA's *Imagine the Universe!*, September 2005, http://imagine.gsfc.nasa.gov/docs /ask_astro/answers/050921a.html.

6. Roger Walsh, "Human Survival: A Psycho-Evolutionary Analysis," *ReVision*, vol 8, no 1 (Summer/Fall 85), 7–10.

7. Derrick Jensen, "The Plants Respond: An Interview with Cleve Backster," *The Sun Magazine*, July 1997, http://thesunmagazine.org/archives/1882.

8. Deepak Chopra, *The Spontaneous Fulfillment of Desire: Harnessing the Infinite Power of Coincidence* (New York: Harmony Books, 2003), 23.

9. Adam Lashinsky, "Larry Page: Google should be like a family," *CNN Money*, January 19, 2012, http://tech.fortune.cnn.com/2012/01/19/best-companies-google-larry-page/.

10. David A. Ebersman, "Facebook: Complete Initial Public Offering," United States Securities and Exchange Commission, February 1, 2012, 70–71, http://www.sec.gov /Archives/edgar/data/1326801/000119312512034517/d287954ds1.htm.

11. Bryan Jaffe, phone interview with Tina Leigh, February 22, 2013.

12. Beth Gardiner, "Business Skills and Buddhist Mindfulness: Some Executive-Education Professors Teach Ways Students Can Calm Their Minds, Increase Focus," *The Wall Street Journal*, April 3, 2012, http://online.wsj.com/article/SB1000142405270230 3816504577305820565167202.html.

13. Eckhart Tolle, homepage, August 2013, http://www.eckharttolle.com/.

Part II

Chapter 5

1. Gail Lynne Goodwin, "Inspiration Archives: Sir Richard Branson," *Inspire Me Today*, http://www.inspiremetoday.com/archiveDisp.php?type=0&ref=1208.

2. Howard Schultz, *Onward: How Starbucks Fought for Its Life without Losing Its Soul* (Emmaus, PA: Rodale Books, 2012).

3. Dan Pink, *A Whole New Mind: Why Right-Brainers Will Rule the Future* (New York: Riverhead Trade, 2006), 158–166.

4. David Herring, "Evolving in the Presence of Fire," *NASA Earth Observatory*, October 1999, http://earthobservatory.nasa.gov/Features/BOREASFire/.

Chapter 6

1. Steve Jobs, "Commencement Speech," June 12, 2005, 15:05, *Stanford Report*, Stanford University, http://news.stanford.edu/news/2005/june15/jobs-061505.html.

2. Glinda the Good Witch, "All you had to do was click your heels three times," *The Wizard of Oz*, Metro-Goldwyn-Mayer, 1939, film.

3. David W. Orme-Johnson, "Preventing Crime Through the Maharishi Effect," *Journal of Offender Rehabilitation*, 35 (2003): 257–281, doi: 10.1300/J076v36n01_12.

4. Ben Obi-Wan Kenobi, "Use the Force," *Star Wars: Episode IV—A New Hope*, Lucas Film, Twentieth Century Fox Film Corporation, 1977, film.

Chapter 7

1. Rhonda Byrne, *The Secret* (New York: Atria, 2002), 16.

Chapter 8

1. Hafiz, Daniel Ladinsky, *The Gift: Poems by Hafiz, the Great Sufi Master* (New York: Penguin Group, 1999), front page epigraph.

2. Anne E. Bromley, "From Accidental Banker to 'Patient Capital' Leader: Distinguished Alumna Describes Creating New Kind of Capitalism," *USAToday*, April 26, 2013, http://news.virginia.edu/content/accidental-banker-patient-capital-leader-distinguished-alumna-describes-creating-new-kind.

3. Jacqueline Novogratz, *The Blue Sweater: Bridging the Gap Between Rich and Poor in an Interconnected World* (Emmaus, PA: Rodale, 2010).

Chapter 9

1. "Chiron," *GreekMytholody.com*, accessed September 9, 2013, http://www.greekmythology.com/Myths/Creatures/Centaur/centaur.html.

2. "Archetypes," *TheChopraCenter.com*, accessed August 2013, http://www.chopra.com/community/online-library/archetypes.

NOTES

Chapter 10

1. Alan Watts, *The Book: On the Taboo Against Knowing Who You Are* (New York: Vintage Books, 1989), 53.

2. Eckhart Tolle, *A New Earth: Awakening to Your Life's Purpose* (New York: Penguin, 2008), 26.

3. "2014 Ford Fusion Hybrid, 'Large or In Charge,'" iSpot.tv, 00:30, from Ford, http://www.ispot.tv/ad/7bBC/2014-ford-fusion-hybrid-large-or-in-charge.

4. Grazyna Fosar and Franz Bludorf, "Scientist Prove DNA Can Be Reprogrammed by Words and Frequencies," *Mind Openerz*, July 17, 2013, http://www.mindopenerz.com/scientist-prove-dna-can-be-reprogrammed-by-words-and-frequencies/.

5. Pico Iyer, "The Value of Suffering," *The New York Times: Sunday Review*, September 7, 2013, http://www.nytimes.com/2013/09/08/opinion/sunday/the-value-of-suffering.html?pagewanted=all&_r=0.

6. "Book of Tens: Jargoniest Jargon We've Heard All Year," *Advertising Age*, December 13, 2010, http://adage.com/article/special-report-the-book-of-tens-2010/advertising-s-jargoniest-jargon/147583/.

7. Fritjof Capra, *The Tao of Physics: An Exploration of the Parallels between Modern Physics and Eastern Mysticism* (Boston: Shambhala, 2010) 132, 143.

Part III
Chapter 11

1. Merriam-Webster, "hero," August 2013 (last accessed), http://www.merriam-webster.com/dictionary/hero.

2. *The Power of Myth*, Bill Moyers and Joseph Campbell, PBS, 1988, http://billmoyers.com/spotlight/download-joseph-campbell-and-the-power-of-myth-audio/.

3. Lao Tzu, *Tao Te Ching* (New York: Vintage Books, 1972), 49.

4. Josh Blatter, "Just one spark," *Roots Rising*, February 2012.

GLOSSARY

abyss the place where we feel we cannot get any lower; our rock bottom; the phase of our journey that helps us see it's time for a change

archetypes in general, the original model or form from which something is made or developed; in the psychology of Carl Jung, a collectively inherited idea or pattern of thought, universally present in our unconscious

call the pull and desire to do something, go somewhere, start a new (ad)venture

collective conscious also called the collective consciousness or collective conscience; a set of shared beliefs, ideas, and modes of thinking that unite society; a way of thinking that makes an individual come to identify with a larger whole (society)

collective unconscious that which collects and organizes the personal experiences (the personal unconscious) that are unique to individuals in a similar way in all species; the part of the unconscious that Jung theorized is genetically determined and occurs in all members of a people or race; the experiences which unite us all

Hero's Journey a pattern of narrative found and named by Joseph Campbell (though the term was coined by James Joyce) that appears in all stories across the world, regardless of time, location, or religion; the journey we all go on in life to fulfill and answer our call

intuitive analytics the ability to engage using strategy and logic while weaving in deep empathy and universal connectivity; mindful and united business interactions

Janus nature Janus is the god of beginnings and transitions in ancient Roman religion and myth; he is almost always depicted as having two faces, one looking to the past and the other toward the future; represents the dichotomous nature in us all

known world the world we are already familiar with; the place and way that we live that may be uncomfortable but is still less uncomfortable than changing, so we stay living in it

left-brain the type of thinking and processing which typically take place in the left cerebral hemisphere of our brains, including but not limited to: logical, verbal, linear, practical, analytical, and sequential

mastery while often confused to mean that one has no more to learn after having reached mastery, this actually means that you are aware of the two worlds, the known and unknown, and can pass between them; you have achieved mastery when you have achieved balance between the material and the spiritual, the known and the unknown

mentors/guides those that the hero meets on his journey that help him, either intentionally or unintentionally, achieve his goal; the people and tools (be they books, websites, exercises, etc.) we find on our journey that will aid us in answering and fulfilling our call

monomyth/über-myth another term for the Hero's Journey as defined and identified by Joseph Campbell

power of *and* what we embrace when we finally realize that we can be two seemingly dichotomous things at the same time and still flourish

right-brain the type of thinking and processing which typically take place in the right cerebral hemisphere of our brains, including but not limited to: intuitive, nonverbal, imaginative, creative, innovative, and holistic

shadow in Jungian psychology, the part of our unconscious that we don't want to accept because we feel like it is bad or dark, but it is really a positive thing to embrace, as even those things we think are dark can truly benefit us

tyranny of *or* what we typically are told by society and suffer under when we feel like we can only be one thing or another and have to choose even if we want to be both

unknown world the world that we are unfamiliar with and are often frightened to enter because it is not something we recognize or understand; the place we need to venture into to truly fulfill our call